SPECIAL MESSAGE TO READERS

THE ULVERSCROFT FOUNDATION
(registered UK charity number 264873)
s established in 1972 to provide funds for
res   ch, diagnosis and treatment of eye diseases.
Examples of major projects funded by
the Ulverscroft Foundation are:-

- The Children's Eye Unit at Moorfields Eye Hospital, London
- The Ulverscroft Children's Eye Unit at Great Ormond Street Hospital for Sick Children
- Funding research into eye diseases and treatment at the Department of Ophthalmology, University of Leicester
- The Ulverscroft Vision Research Group, Institute of Child Health
- Twin operating theatres at the Western Ophthalmic Hospital, London
- The Chair of Ophthalmology at the Royal Australian College of Ophthalmologists

You can help further the work of the Foundation by making a donation or leaving a legacy.
Every contribution is gratefully received. If you would like to help support the Foundation or require further information, please contact:

THE ULVERSCROFT FOUNDATION
The Green, Bradgate Road, Anstey
Leicester LE7 7FU, England
Tel: (0116) 236 4325

website: v  t.com

D0510185

Josephine Reynolds was the first ever woman to join the Fire Service full-time in the UK. After falling in love with fellow firefighter David Blakeney, an ex-French Foreign Legion fighter, the pair married and headed to the Amazon to continue their adventurous life together.

FIRE WOMAN

When seventeen-year-old Josephine Reynolds signed up to the Norfolk Fire Service in 1982, there was no such thing as a firefighter — only firemen. Nevertheless, she was determined to stick it out. From the gruelling fifteen months of training — wrestling 25-metre thrashing, water-spurting hoses, and manoeuvring through pitch-dark, smoke-filled rooms — to her years on the job as a fully-fledged firefighter — tackling forest fires, escaped zoo animals and unexploded bombs — she tells the story of the exhaustion and exhilaration, the grief and camaraderie, of her career with Britain's Fire Service.

JOSEPHINE REYNOLDS

◆

FIRE WOMAN

The Extraordinary Story of Britain's
First Female Firefighter

Complete and Unabridged

ULVERSCROFT
Leicester

First published in Great Britain in 2017 by
Michael O'Mara Books Limited
London

First Large Print Edition
published 2017
by arrangement with
Michael O'Mara Books Limited
London

Some names of certain individuals in this book
have been changed to protect their privacy.

A catalogue record for this book is available
from the British Library.

ISBN 978–1–4448–3445–1

Published by
F. A. Thorpe (Publishing)
Anstey, Leicestershire

Set by Words & Graphics Ltd.
Anstey, Leicestershire
Printed and bound in Great Britain by
T. J. International Ltd., Padstow, Cornwall

This book is printed on acid-free paper

This book is for you —
the brave and the bold.

The misfits.

Let your light shine brightly.

Contents

1

Burning Down the House

I was twelve years old when our house burned down.

We lived at the bottom of a hill in deepest, darkest West Wales, but most days it felt as if the four of us — me, my mum, my stepfather Ben and my younger brother Malcy — had fallen off the edge of the world completely. I'd only ever lived in small villages before we'd moved to Wales, and had never been to a large town, let alone seen the bright lights. Each night I would lie in bed in my flannel nightie praying that something — anything — would happen. But this wasn't what I'd had in mind.

I woke up in a bedroom filled with suffocating black smoke. Through the haze, I could just make out the figure of Ben frantically hammering on the wooden window frame, yelling, 'Jo, Jo, wake up, the house is on fire!' Considering his usual form of communication was a grunt, I sensed that it must be something serious.

From that moment on, I felt like I was

playing a part in a film. One minute I was choking and spluttering as Ben lifted me through the window and put me down with a bump on the cold damp earth outside. The next, he was shouting, 'Don't worry, Mum and Malcy are safe, stay here!' as he sprinted off to the red phone box at the bottom of the hill to dial 999. Fifteen minutes later, amid the sort of flashing lights I'd only ever seen on *Star Wars*, two bright red fire engines pulled up outside. From within emerged a group of rugged strangers carrying hoses and ladders who set about extinguishing the blaze with grim determination. I sat transfixed. Who were these silent superheroes?

When the blaze was finally extinguished, I sat with my mum as she stared at the smouldering remains. Her prized collection of Elvis records had melted away — all that was left was the charred sleeve of 'GI Blues', scattered in the debris. 'Don't worry, Jo-Jo, everything will be all right,' she said, as the smoke cleared and we were drawn together in one of those moments you never forget. I didn't cry when I realized that my own few meagre possessions were now part of the glowing embers. Deep down, though, I knew that something inside me had changed.

★　★　★

My mum Marian was a fiery Scorpio — light the fuse and stand well back. Her Titian-red hair, ivory complexion and hourglass figure could literally stop the traffic. One day when we were out in Narberth, the sight of her walking along in her skin-tight purple jumpsuit caused a motorist to drive straight into a lamppost.

Six feet tall with black hair and blue eyes, my dad Michael looked like he'd stepped out of a Brylcreem ad. His good looks and easy smile disguised a hair-trigger temper, but love is blind and this myopic pair stumbled up the aisle at Albury Town Hall in Hertfordshire in March 1963. She was seventeen and he was twenty-one. I came along two years later, arriving at 1 p.m. on Mother's Day, 28 March 1965, which makes me an Aries — a fire sign.

My parents' local pub was called The Catherine Wheel, but most of the fireworks took place at our house. Anything could spark a display, but most of the friction revolved around the car. Dad was a mechanic at Laurie Newton's, the local garage, and when Mum returned home from work in her grey Morris 1000, he would inspect the car for damage. Even the tiniest scratch could send him into a rage, and if she was five minutes late, an interrogation worthy of the Spanish Inquisition would start. Mum could be every bit as jealous and aggressive herself, and usually gave as good as she got.

The highlight of our weekend would be Saturday afternoon, when we would visit our grandparents' house for tea. Me and Malcy would sit on the sofa watching the wrestling, staring agog as Big Daddy tackled bad guys like Kendo Nagasaki and Mick McManus. This would act as a cue for wrestling bouts of our own, rolling around on the living-room floor until one of us signalled for the other to stop.

Unfortunately, there were no such rules for the fights at home. One evening I watched from the top of the stairs as Mum and Dad had another screaming fight just as Grandad Reynolds — who was shell-shocked from the First World War — had a panic attack. *The Waltons* it was not. Thankfully I wasn't alone in this madhouse, and my brother Malcy, our little dog Sad Eyes and I became our own pre-school support group for each other.

The dysfunctional union between my parents couldn't last, and aided by a friend Mum had met while working at the local greengrocer's, she packed our bags one day while Dad was out at work. From the moment the front door slammed shut behind us, life took on the sensation of one long rollercoaster ride. We moved constantly for the next few years, and the endless packing and unpacking of boxes soon began to feel perfectly normal.

By the time I was seven, to put some distance between herself and Dad, Mum had moved us from Cambridgeshire to West Wales, where she married a local builder called Ben Morris. One day while out driving in Ben's red Capri the pair of them drove past a dilapidated cottage for sale. They fell in love with it, and before any repairs could start the four of us were swiftly installed.

'This is our new home, Jo-Jo, we're not gypsies any more!' Mum said as I stepped over the debris-strewn threshold. Stability at last! Or so I thought. When work was finally completed on our new home, much to my horror they decided to combine their names and christen it Ben-y-Mar (it was a Welsh thing, apparently). It was the tackiest idea I'd ever heard. If it sounded like a holiday camp, believe me it wasn't.

Every night we would have to prepare a meal for Mum and Ben on their return from work. Before long we had a repertoire to rival the Galloping Gourmet. Main courses would include gammon steaks, burgers, fish fingers, sausages and pies, all served with chips or mash. Puddings would centre around our favourites: tinned peaches with condensed milk, mashed bananas and custard or butterscotch Angel Delight. Many times, Malcy's role as sous chef at the Reynolds Bistro would get too much, and he'd hurl the washing-up bowl, complete with dirty water and potato peelings, all over me. 'Jo-Jo darling, could you make me a cup of tea?' my mum would call through from the sitting room, as I desperately tried to restore order.

In the summer we'd be on garden detail. I can still recall a seven-year-old Malcy struggling to push the lawnmower around the garden as I weeded the vegetable patch, both of us under strict instructions not to disturb Mum as she lay sunbathing. Had there been a labour union for the under-tens we might have had a way to fight back. As it was, any pocket money would be hard earned, and usually splurged on bags of sweets, washed down with homemade ginger beer from a plastic pump in the immersion cupboard.

Being waited on hand and foot never seemed to improve Ben's mood. A born sulker, he was grumpy if he couldn't go to The Bush, the pub down the road, every night, and even grumpier when he did. This, added to Mum's acute jealousy of other women, ensured there was always an atmosphere simmering along with the chip pan on the stove.

My own relationship with Mum was strained at the best of times. When we were younger we'd spend idyllic afternoons with her, enjoying picnics on Tenby beach and wandering through the slate quarries in the Preseli Mountains. But after she met Ben, her controlling ways became more extreme. It was only when we stayed at my friend Pearl's house for six weeks after the fire at Ben-y-Mar that I realized things could be different. Coming home from school would be a time to have fun, feed the chickens, play badminton and watch *Top of the Pops*. Pearl's mum happily cooked dinner, singing along to the radio. It was another world.

When the renovation of our home was finally complete, Mum announced that they would be renting it out during the summer months to tourists. This would mean the four of us living in the caravan at the end of the garden until the holiday season was over. The thought of being squeezed into such a confined space with my family horrified me. I'd already heard too much of Ben's drunken snoring. To his credit, Ben came up with a solution — he bought me an old builder's shed to live in. I painted the walls my favourite shade of green and it became my refuge throughout the summer. I can still remember the thrill of announcing 'I'm off to the shed'. It was my first taste of independence and I savoured every drop.

During the winter, my only escape was on Saturday nights. While my mum, Ben and Malcy would be in the sitting room glued to *The Professionals*, I would sit alone in the kitchen and watch *Dallas* on the tiny portable black and white TV. I was bewitched by the beautiful people, the fabulous clothes, the glamour. Why couldn't my life be like that?

Despite the chaos of our family life, I somehow managed to pass my eleven-plus. I prayed that was my ticket out.

* * *

School days are the best days of your life. Whoever thought that phrase up must have had a warped sense of humour.

With the country still parched from the hottest summer on record, I started at Whitland Grammar School in September 1976. Up until that point, my fashion pointers had come from Mum's favourite retailer, Oxfam. So it was daunting to be marched into Narberth one boiling hot Saturday afternoon for a shopping trip the week before term started. 'Do we really need all this stuff?' I asked, worried about how much it had all cost as we left the school outfitters weighed down with the uniform required for my new life: navy skirt, red shirt, red socks, navy and red striped tie, leather satchel and a blazer with a badge emblazoned with a picture of a sheep and the motto *I fyny for nod* (Aim for the highest). What on earth had I got myself into?

My trepidation at what lay ahead only grew on my first day. I had decided to jazz up my new outfit with some clumsily applied makeup. As I clambered aboard the school bus one of the sixth-form boys looked me up and down and in lilting tones asked, 'Are you a prostitute?' I had no idea what he meant, but I had a feeling it wasn't a compliment. Things only got worse when, forty-five minutes later, we pulled up outside what looked like a Victorian workhouse. Here I came face to face with my new classmates, who all seemed to be half my height and talking in some unintelligible language. Mercifully, there was one other English girl in my year, Claire Sturgess. We towered over everyone in assembly, our beanpole frames shaking with suppressed laughter as the dour headmaster, Mr Bancroft, led sombre recitals of the Lord's Prayer in Welsh.

The strict rules about which subjects boys and girls could study infuriated me. The boys did woodwork and metalwork; the girls did

9

cooking and sewing. Why should the boys have all the fun? It was time to make a stand. 'I won't be attending your class again, miss,' I announced one Tuesday afternoon to our home economics teacher. If I thought that was the end of it, I had another think coming. The next morning I was duly summoned to the office of Mr Bancroft. A brooding heavy-set figure in a flowing black gown, he ruled the school through liberal use of the cane. 'Who, exactly, do you think you are, Josephine?' he said, before lecturing me on how no pupil had ever dared challenge the status quo in Whitland's hundred-year history. This girl was not for turning, however, and after much huffing and puffing from the powers that be it was agreed I could take up my place amid the sawdust and wood glue. It was music to my ears. Before long I had made a beautiful rosewood jewellery box, which acted as a handy peace offering for my mum after one of our many rows.

Most of the time I would daydream through lessons, mesmerized by the bright red lipstick smeared on the teeth of our language teacher, Fanny French, as she chuntered through the curriculum.

My greatest dread was reserved for PE, especially hockey. At Whitland they took this barbaric variant on sport seriously, and the state-of-the-art red gravel pitch seemed designed to soak up the blood of rival teams, who would leave with their shins bleeding and battered after an encounter with the strapping home team. In the third year, my lack of interest in choosing my O-level options was greeted with tuts and raised eyebrows. While my classmates were aiming to be the next generation of doctors, lawyers and teachers, this girl just wanted to earn money and have fun. Their constant talk about going to the 'right' university was as alien to me as the playground chat about family skiing trips, and I felt no one understood my desire to enter the world of work.

My quiet declaration that I had no interest in going to university was met with a stony silence by our careers advisor, Miss Jones. 'Well, Josephine, there's always the army,' she said flatly. Was that really all that was available to me? The Falklands War was being waged, and I had no intention of grappling with Argentinian conscripts at Goose Green. What other options were there? And, more importantly, how exactly was I going to stay sane for the next three years at Whitland?

Here's my diary entry for 28 November 1979:

Today I put salt in Malcy's tea because he really annoyed me. Mum made me drink it and told me I wasn't allowed out of the house for a week, and no pocket money. Heard Pink Floyd's 'Another Brick in the Wall' tonight on the John Peel show. It blew my mind. Anarchy is coming!

Something inside me was stirring. The world was changing and so was I.

2

Teenage Kicks

I think his name was David. To be honest I didn't care. I was kissing a boy for the first time and it felt great. Better than great. We'd been pogo-ing to The Police's 'Roxanne', and now we were holding hands and pledging eternal love. We were at the local disco at Tavernspite, but I felt like I was Bianca Jagger riding through Studio 54 on a white horse.

Of course, I never saw him again. What really mattered — sorry, David — was that the real Jo had arrived and taken over. Because from the moment I turned fourteen suddenly there was no stopping me. I no longer cared about Mum's moods and the torrent of rubbish I was dealing with at home. With my first pay packet I triumphantly bought a pair of black PVC trousers. It was time for sex, drugs and rock 'n' roll! Which was easier said than done in rural Wales.

The nearest thing to a teeming metropolis was Haverfordwest, a fifteen-minute bus ride away along the A40. I was waitressing in the Harfat café there when I met Robin. Perhaps it was just my PVC trousers, but we were soon being young punks together. Robin's scrawny frame was topped by spiky peroxided hair, and dancing around in his pipe-cleaner jeans he looked like one of the punk rockers I'd seen on *Top of the Pops*. Either that or he'd seen a ghost. Robin was the son of the local undertaker and we'd spend the afternoons watching his dad embalm his latest client. Clearly, I'd hit dating pay-dirt. My evenings would be spent hunched in the cellar watching Robin's band rehearse. He would strum his guitar furiously with one skinny leg resting on a half-built coffin, as he barked out songs by Stiff Little Fingers. His rendition of 'Barbed Wire Love' was enough to wake the dead. But I didn't hang around long enough to find out.

And then I met Rupert. The coolest kid for miles around, or at least in my book, he exuded a public-schoolboy confidence that was new to me. Better still, he could recite the lyrics to every Siouxsie and The Banshees B-side. I fancied him like crazy.

We met when I was working as kitchen maid at the local country house hotel his parents owned. 'Hey babe, do you want to come upstairs and see my etchings?' he'd say with an ironic smile when I finished my shift. How could I resist?

We'd spend our afternoons holed up in his room, singing along to The Cure and smoking spliffs from the cannabis plants he secretly grew in the hotel's garden. It was pure bliss. The two of us had rebellion in common and, as things progressed, I would climb out of my bedroom window and walk up the hill in the dead of night to meet him. Sadly these midnight trysts came to an end when my mum found out about us and gave us a humiliating public dressing-down in front of his mother and father.

Other nights, I'd go to the local Cross Hands disco with my girlfriends where I'd model my new wardrobe — a black and white mini-dress, fishnet tights and a pair of kitten heels. We'd all dance like mad things to The Specials' 'Too Much Too Young' while drinking Cinzano and lemonade laced with cigarette ash. 'It'll get us drunk more quickly,' I'd announce, having learned this vital life tip from the letters page of *Jackie*. Deep down, I knew this was as good as it was going to get if I stayed. I'd already had a glimpse of life beyond the borders when Malcy and I would go and see my dad and his new wife Jean during the school holidays.

Like Dorothy in *The Wizard of Oz*, the world seemed to switch from black and white to colour the minute we changed buses at

London Victoria. I'd never been to a city before and I was spellbound — the lights, the cars, the buildings, the people — it was beyond exciting.

However, these trips would only make things worse on my return to Ben-y-Mar. Mum and I would row constantly, or ignore each other completely. One of these long uncomfortable silences was finally broken the week before my sixteenth birthday. 'So what do you want for your birthday, then?' she said. 'I want to leave home,' I snapped. It was a solution that worked for both of us. Sure enough, on the morning of 28 March 1981 I came downstairs to find a neatly wrapped vintage suitcase on the sitting-room floor. I hated leaving Malcy behind, but I was desperate to escape. It was time to spread my wings.

*   *   *

I've no idea what my dad and Jean made of me turning up on the doorstep of their house at 49 Eastern Road in Norwich the week after I'd taken my O-levels. Maybe they were secretly expecting me. Either way, my transformation from shy country girl to life and soul of the party had finally begun.

My new partner in crime was my

16

stepbrother Graeme. Six foot two in his smelly socks, he dressed like a wannabe Ramone in skinny t-shirts and drainpipe jeans, and had the attitude to match. Our evenings would be spent touring the local pubs in his old Ford Zephyr with the zeal of sailors on shore leave. After all my dormant years in Wales, it felt like life had finally begun. Going to see bands play live at UEA was an even bigger eye-opener. The college kids looked impossibly cool. Did they do those wacky asymmetrical haircuts themselves, or did they go to a salon?

I loved jumping around to The Stranglers, and yelling 'Jean-Jacques, I love you!' at sexy bassist Jean-Jacques Burnel, as I gulped down pints of cider and took deep breaths of the stale, cigarette-tinged air. As we hurtled home through the city centre with The Ramones 'I Wanna Be Sedated' blaring from the cassette radio, no seat belt, I was at my most ragingly alive.

Despite all this fun, the question of my future still hung in the air like a black cloud. To buy some time I got a job waitressing at The Oaklands Hotel a mile down the road. To my horror this job required me to wear an old-fashioned black and white French maid's outfit. So much for female emancipation — but it certainly helped with the tips!

17

I knew I needed to get a 'proper' job sooner rather than later, and my afternoons off would be spent scouring the jobs pages of the *Eastern Evening News*. I was also applying for police cadet courses across the country. I had no real desire to join what Malcy still insisted on calling 'The Fuzz', but I wasn't sure what else to do. I had barely scraped together four O-levels. Yet from Birmingham to Bristol to London, no matter which force I contacted, the message was the same: 'We are no longer recruiting; please try again in six months.'

My world was contracting. It was during one of these soul-destroying sessions scouring the Situations Vacant columns that I chanced upon an advert requesting applications for a trainee firefighter course. 'What do you think, should I apply?' I asked Graeme as we sat around the kitchen table. He didn't say anything before launching into a rousing rendition of the theme tune to *Trumpton*: 'Pugh, Pugh, Barney McGrew, Cuthbert, Dibble, Grub.'

'What will my mum think?' I asked, ignoring him. 'Don't worry about your mum,' he replied, 'she's crazy.' I knew Dad would be supportive. He had worked as a fireman at

Stansted airport, and he'd proudly shown me photos of him looking young and dashing in uniform. My decision was made — I was going to apply.

The next morning I went to work as usual dressed in my French maid's outfit. Little did I know, as I dropped my application into the postbox in the pouring rain, it was exactly what one man was waiting for.

★ ★ ★

As Chief Fire Officer for Norfolk, Bruce Hogg had the sort of autonomy his peers in London dreamed about. A progressive thinker with twenty years' good service behind him, Hogg saw the opportunity to launch an initiative that would bring the fire service into line with the other emergency services. At the monthly meeting of the heads of the Norfolk Fire Service, he proposed a pilot scheme aimed at sixteen-year-old school leavers. Instead of completing the usual twelve weeks of training, they would embark on an extended fifteen-month training scheme. This would both fast-track recruits with the potential to be officer material and add a batch of young, dynamic individuals to the ranks.

The scheme should also, Hogg insisted, be open to both boys and girls. His thinking wasn't entirely altruistic. When the media got hold of it, Hogg reasoned, the ensuing press would only reflect well on the Norfolk Fire Service. All that the scheme needed in order to work was the right person to apply. Needless to say, I was blissfully unaware of all this intrigue. In fact, my knowledge of the fire service added up to a big fat zilch.

I couldn't believe my eyes when the letter arrived at Eastern Road telling me I'd got an interview.

The night before the big day, I decided I ought to do some homework. Who knows, there might be a written test? Best be prepared. I had found a dusty-looking book about the fire service in our local library, and asked Graeme to quiz me on it.

'When was the Metropolitan Fire Service formed?' he said in his most bored voice as we sat side by side on the bed in my cramped attic room. 'Easy — 1868,' I replied confidently. 'Incorrect,' he said with a grin. 'The answer is 1866, *SIR*! And we'll have no more of that insubordination here, Reynolds. You're not hanging around with your waster punk friends now!' After a swift but brutal pillow fight, I gave up on the prospect of getting any help.

After we'd said goodnight, I lay in bed staring blankly at the ceiling. While Graeme and I got on well, his life had little or no structure. This was partly why we were such good mates. But I also knew that if I played my cards right, my life was about to become highly regimented. Would our friendship be able to take the strain? I also prayed I wouldn't be the only girl being interviewed. I'd been the odd one out all my life, and desperately hoped that HMS *Reynolds* wasn't about to set off on another lonely voyage.

*　*　*

A twenty-five-minute drive from Norwich, Wymondham Fire Station was so isolated it might as well have been on the moon. The moment I arrived, I knew that all my worst fears were about to be confirmed. Having been ushered towards a car park, which a uniformed man referred to as the 'drill yard', I found myself standing in line with fifty boys, all of whom radiated the cocksure attitude that seems to appear naturally the day boys turn sixteen.

They were all, I noted with dismay, staring at me as if I was the first woman they'd ever seen. As their eyes bored into me, looking at me curiously like mountain gorillas clapping eyes on David Attenborough, I could actually feel my nerves jangling. This was starting to

21

feel like a huge mistake. To make matters worse, it soon became clear that rather than having to undertake a written examination, we were going to be put through a series of physical tests.

After we had been split up into four groups, I took my place in line and watched as the first of the boys were put through their paces by our stony-faced instructors. Not only was I not going to be interviewed, it looked like I was now a participant in the Sports Day From Hell. Having changed into the PE kit we were asked to bring with us, I was still trying to scrub some of the makeup from my face when I was called on to attempt the first activity. This involved climbing to the top of a 12-metre ladder positioned against a concrete construction called the Training Tower. Once up there, I had to lean backwards and fling my arms outwards in a 'star' shape, holding on to the ladder with just my ankles in what was called a 'leg lock' for thirty seconds. That's right, I had to let go with my hands! Ten minutes earlier, I'd been standing there minding my own business. Now, I was dangling 40 feet up in the air, as if it was perfectly normal.

As I stretched backwards, supported by nothing but my right leg, my world was literally turned upside down. Far below me I could see the other candidates running around like tiny ants. A surge of sheer exhilaration coursed through my nervous system. Maybe this wasn't going to be so bad after all? Little did I know what was to come.

For our next test, we had to complete a 100-metre dash in less than sixty seconds. Easy, you might think. Except that we had to do it carrying a 75-kilogram canvas sand dummy across our shoulders in a 'fireman's lift'. To give you some idea of how heavy this was, the average holiday suitcase weighs approximately 25 kilograms. Not only was it three times heavier than that, it was also stiff, unbending and designed to replicate the dead weight of the human body.

I'd seen some of the boys struggle even to lift it, and as my turn approached I knew it was make-or-break time. On the command, 'Next candidate, go!' I summoned all of my inner strength and hauled the dummy up from the tarmac and onto my skinny shoulders.

As my shoulders began to throb, every fibre of my being told me this wasn't one of my better ideas. Not only did I have to carry this bloody thing, I had to run with it against the clock! After 50 metres, my legs started to wobble. I knew that the sight of my stick-thin frame practically bent double under the crippling weight of this human-shaped monstrosity must have looked utterly ridiculous. What the hell, I thought. Any dignity and grace I had started the day with had long since vanished, and I was determined I wasn't going to give up.

As I staggered on, I gained strength from imagining them back in the mess room, chortling at the memory of seeing me fall flat on my face. Well, sorry to disappoint you, guys, I said to myself through gritted teeth, that ain't going to happen. As I crossed the finishing line and heaved the sand dummy onto the tarmac, I saw the instructor's stopwatch click on one minute exactly. If I was expecting garlands and champagne, however, I quickly realized I was mistaken. 'Next candidate, go!' was his only response, as I raised myself off my knees. Thankfully, judging by the shell-shocked looks on the boys' faces, I wasn't the only one struggling to negotiate this brutally steep learning curve. Like a scene from a documentary about a Club 18–30 trip to Magaluf, everywhere I turned I saw lads looking dazed or puking in the grass verge. With a kind of mute hopelessness, I steeled myself for the third test.

Thankfully, this one was more straightforward. We were each handed a bulky cylindrical hose and ordered to 'run out' a 25-metre length across the drill yard as quickly as possible. This was a straight sprint, timed at the far end by another stony-faced instructor (where did they get them from?) with a stopwatch.

The best was saved until last, however. Having each been given a rubber face mask with the eyes blacked out, we were ordered to crawl through a makeshift tunnel, 20 metres long, made up of old wooden storage pallets and covered with a thick black tarpaulin. To any passers-by, the sight of fifty boys and a single girl emerging from the other end, sweaty, dishevelled and breathing heavily must have been quite alarming.

I would later learn that these were all carefully thought-out tests, designed to push us to our limits and expose our weaknesses. Specifically, they were being used to assess — in this order — our ability to deal with heights, gauge our strength and stamina, monitor our physical fitness and see how we coped in confined spaces.

The strict, disciplinarian approach of the instructors was no accident, either. This was designed to weed out anyone with a problem with authority and find those recruits with a certain mental attitude. As I would learn soon enough, the fire service was all about being able to take orders, no matter how ridiculous they might seem. In this respect, I later discovered, the fire service had a lot in common with the Navy. Not only did they share many of the same drills, but like sailors, firemen could typically spend days or weeks without doing anything much at all. However, when the moment came, they had to be able to rise to the challenge and act decisively in an instant. Even without knowing any of this, my own mindset had changed as the day had gone on. I'd started off thinking that the whole thing was faintly ridiculous — actually, scratch that, more like bloody ridiculous — as well as insanely difficult. By the end of it, however, I felt utterly exhausted but also strangely exhilarated. As we were dismissed at the end of the day and I watched the instructors walk off together, laughing and joking at all the things they'd witnessed, I felt a pang of envy pierce my gut with almost physical force. I desperately wanted to become part of their world and get to know all of its strange practices.

* * *

'So, how did it go?' asked my dad eagerly when I made it back home to Eastern Road. I was too tired to speak, and shrugged as I

26

made my way upstairs to my room and flung myself on the bed. From the kitchen, I could tell that Jean was making her signature dish — sausages and mash with Bisto gravy and boiled cabbage — and my mind began to drift as the comforting smell of fried onions wafted through the house. Could I really become a firefighter? I'd been able to complete all the physical challenges they'd thrown at me, and I'd even coped with heights far better than most of the boys, some of whom had been reduced to gibbering wrecks when left to dangle forty feet in the air.

My thoughts were rudely interrupted by the arrival in my room of Graeme. 'Well, spill the beans then!' he said, elbowing me in the ribs so that we could sit side by side on the bed.

'It was bloody hard work, but I loved every minute,' I said, trying to convey how it had been the most thrillingly horrible day of my life. 'I was the only girl there, though, so it's hard to tell if I did well or not. There might be hundreds of other girls turning up on another day for all I know.'

'Yes, but they won't be Jo Reynolds, will they?' he said with a grin.

A few days later, I'd just come back from doing the afternoon shift at work when I noticed a brown envelope waiting for me on the kitchen table. I ripped it open. Inside was an invitation to attend a follow-up interview the following week at Whitegates, the fire brigade headquarters at Hethersett.

I burst into a huge smile just as Graeme walked into the room.

'I told you, didn't I?' he said, beaming.

★　★　★

Set back off the A11, Whitegates was by far and away the most impressive building I'd ever been to. An imposing eighteenth-century building positioned at the end of a sweeping drive, its wisteria-covered walls seemed to carry the weight of history.

Walking through the heavy oak door at the main entrance, I noticed a long polished corridor leading to a grand central staircase, along which fire service personnel in full uniform and smartly dressed administrative staff went about their business with brisk efficiency. I looked down at my white shirt, black skirt and matching black shoes — all of which I used in my waitressing job — and thanked God I'd made the effort to look as smart as possible.

Having turned left into the reception area, I waited patiently as the woman behind the counter looked for my name on the list of interviewees. 'Ah, yes . . . Miss Reynolds,' she said, handing me a name tag as I signed and dated the registration book. 'Could you wait outside in the hall, please? You'll be called when it's your time to go upstairs.' As I sat down, the sense of propriety and order I felt was almost overwhelming. Somehow, the venerable history of the entire fire service had seeped through the walls of Whitegates. Opposite where I was sitting, highly polished glass cabinets gave a glimpse of the proud tradition of the Norfolk Fire Service. Drawn by an almost magnetic impulse, I found myself scrutinizing their contents. On the top shelf of the first cabinet was the brigade's emblem, an eight-pointed star known as the Cross of St John. Originally used by the Knights of St John of Jerusalem at the time of the Crusades and commonly known as the Maltese Cross, its eight tenets were said to represent the knightly virtues: tact, perseverance, gallantry, loyalty, dexterity, explicitness, observation and sympathy. Beneath it, a display card explained that it had been appropriated by the Norfolk Fire Service as these were all qualities required by a fireman.

In the next cabinet along, something even more remarkable caught my eye. On the second shelf down I noticed a beautifully framed British Empire Medal for gallantry awarded to Divisional Officer James William Todd for his actions during a fire at RAF Neatishead in February 1966. As I peered at it, I saw my reflection in the glass, and felt a shiver run through me. Suddenly, it hit me. Here was an occupation that demanded the whole of me; not just my physical presence at a certain place and time. This was a job that required total commitment and a dedication to duty that few jobs could match. These people were risking their lives to save others and help their community. I desperately wanted to be a part of it.

Ten minutes later, I wasn't so sure. Having been ushered upstairs, I'd found myself in what looked like the drawing room of a country house. But quite the opposite to a convivial dinner, I found myself sitting nervously on a hard-backed chair opposite Norfolk Fire Service's eight most senior officers, all of whom were giving me their best poker-faced stare.

This was it. I realized that what happened in the next half an hour could completely change my life. I looked out of the window and watched a pair of magpies fly by. What was that nursery rhyme? 'One for sorrow, two for joy'? Maybe this could be my day after all.

'So, Jo . . . what makes you think you

belong in the fire service?' said a man who introduced himself as Divisional Officer Bennison. As the questions came at me thick and fast, I rattled off my pre-prepared answers, making sure I spoke as clearly and confidently as I could, bearing in mind my heart was racing and my insides had turned to jelly.

'Do you really think you've got the physical strength to handle this type of work?'

'What attributes do you think you will bring to the job?'

'How will you manage working alongside men all the time?'

On it went for forty minutes. Just when I thought the interrogation had come to an end, there was one final question. It was delivered by a man who had been silent up until now — Chief Fire Officer Hogg. 'Why should we invest our time and money in you, when later on in life, you might have, shall we say, different priorities?' he said, leaning forwards in his chair.

I let the question hang in the air as I thought of how best to answer it. What on earth did he mean? Was he suggesting that, as a female, I was only interested in getting married and having babies? I wasn't sure, so decided to play it safe, just in case. 'Well, sir,' I said, trying to remain as non-committal as possible, 'if you train me correctly, then that shouldn't be a problem.'

What I really wanted to say was that there was nothing else I would rather do than commit myself to this most noble of professions. Give me a chance, I wanted to say, as I fixed him with my most can-do smile. Give me an opportunity and I'll be the best firefighter you've ever seen. I'll climb ladders, I'll scrub floors, I'll even make the bloody tea if that's what it takes to become part of this organization. Because I've never wanted anything more in my life and I'll work every minute of every day to make the grade. I was shaken from my reverie by the sound of Chief Fire Officer Hogg's voice. 'Thank you. That will be all, Miss Reynolds.'

*   *   *

How had I done? The truth was, I hadn't a clue. I knew there were places for only six candidates, and as the weeks passed, it felt as though the whole of my future life hung in the balance.

Finally, on the morning of 23 May 1982 I came home from work to see another brown envelope waiting for me on the kitchen table. 'You've either won the premium bonds or this is from your friends in the fire brigade,' said my dad as he handed it to me. I'd spent the last six hours making beds, plumping pillows and cleaning bathrooms while listening to guests complain about their faulty teasmade. I wasn't in the mood for more bad news.

'I can't open it. Can you do it for me, please?' I said, as I passed the envelope to my dad with shaking hands.

'You'd better sit down,' he said, examining the contents. 'You've only gone and done it.'

I was in. In my excitement I rang Ben's brother Johnny, a Sub Officer at Pembroke Dock Fire Station. 'Can I be the first to tell you that you're entering a world of pain?' he said with smug satisfaction. 'Even for the blokes it's really hard to carry someone down a ladder. Trust me, Jo, it's not going to be easy.' Well, like they say — there's nothing like families to bring you back down to earth.

The truth was, I didn't care. I'd been accepted by the fire service and felt I could handle anything that would be thrown at me. The *plain* truth was that for all my bravado, I didn't have a clue what I had let myself in for when I reported for duty at 9 a.m. sharp on a glorious July morning in 1982.

3

Welcome to the Pleasuredome

I'd left Wales, passed my driving test and got a job in arguably the most noble and loved profession in the world. From now on, I fantasized, my days would be spent basking in the company of hunky six-foot heroes.

I was therefore a little taken aback on my first day when I was met by a balding middle-aged man. He was dressed in a pair of sagging denim dungarees and had a face best described as 'lived-in'. 'I'm Ralph the caretaker,' he said in a broad Norfolk accent, mumbling to himself as he shuffled towards me with a tray of cheese rolls and iced buns. 'You must be one of the new recruits — or the latest shower of shit, as I call them,' he said, scowling. 'You do know that half of every new intake fail to make it, don't you?'

My confidence had already been shaken by this reception, and it was knocked further by the arrival of the other five male recruits followed by a shaven-headed instructor with a murderous look in his eyes. Instantly I felt the temperature drop a couple of degrees. This

34

guy clearly wasn't going to take any prisoners. 'What in God's name do you call that?' he bellowed at the first boy in line, gesturing at his elaborate coiffure. 'Didn't your mum read you the letter telling you to get your hair cut before you showed up here?' As the boy lowered his eyes in humiliation, his tormentor directed his gaze at his next victim, a mop-headed youth called Stuart Jeneson. 'And that goes for you, too, Worzel. Get your backside down to the barbers NOW!'

It was 9.01 on my first day and I was beginning to realize that the next fifteen months were going to feel like an eternity. 'As for the rest of you,' he roared, 'get your skinny little arses down to the Stores and pick up your uniforms. On the double!'

I could tell from the shell-shocked expressions on the faces of my fellow trainees that they weren't expecting quite such a rude introduction either. But this didn't stop us all scampering down the corridors as though our lives depended on it, where we were met by a man in his early sixties with a twinkle in his eye. This was Bob.

'Ah, so you're the Trainee Reynolds I've heard so much about,' he said in the sort of cockney accent I'd previously only heard on episodes of *The Sweeney*. 'We've never had a female recruit before, but I've been given all your measurements,' he said with a wink. Thank God I haven't got big boobs, I said to myself, as he piled up my brand new firefighter's uniform in neat piles on the large wooden counter in front of him.

Look out Gianni Versace, this is my collection for 1982. Formal wear: black shoes, black socks, black trousers, black belt, black blazer, black clip-on tie, black cap. Leisurewear: navy blue trousers, navy blue t-shirt, navy blue jumper. On top of all that, the Haute Couture collection — my firefighting kit, consisting of knee-high steel-toecap wellies, yellow plastic leggings, heavy black wool jacket and bright yellow cork helmet. All of these, of course, came in men's shapes and sizes, but I really didn't care. I could hardly believe it was all for me.

* * *

In the minibus that took us from Hethersett to our training base at Wymondham, I silently ran the rule over my fellow trainees. It was good news. Despite all the testosterone flying around, I felt I could hold my own. Aside from Neil Dallas and Stuart Jeneson — who both sheepishly turned up later looking like they'd been attacked by a lawnmower — there were three other boys on the scheme:

Matthew Caston, Ray Harcourt and Stewart Graveling.

Each radiated some kind of 'attitude'. Matthew was cocksure enough to show up on a brand new VF 750cc Yamaha motorbike. Ray oozed a rockabilly surliness and wore — nice touch — pink fluorescent socks. Stewart had the devilish grin of a born joker. As the minibus pulled up outside Wymondham Fire Station, it was obvious this was where the hard work started. A gloomy low-rise building set adrift in the Norfolk countryside, it was a far cry from the olde worlde grandeur of Whitegates. Still holding our kit, we were marched into a classroom on the ground floor where two men in full dress uniform were standing in front of a blackboard overlooking the drill yard.

'Good morning, junior firefighters. My name is Leading Fireman Holmes, and this is Sub Officer Zipfel,' said the younger of the two men in the kind of humorous tone which suggested that he, at least, wasn't a *complete* bastard. 'This will be your home for the next fifteen months. From this point on, you are neither male nor female, you are trainee firefighters. Impossible as it may seem, we will attempt to make something resembling a firefighter out of you. Through some incredible stroke of luck, or, more likely, someone's terrible mistake, you all managed to pass the interview. However, just remember there are hundreds of other candidates who didn't make it. If you don't make the grade during the first four weeks, we have plenty more highly credible candidates who would be delighted to take your place.' He cleared his throat. The niceties, I suspected, were over. 'Right, now wake up, get changed into your PT kit and we'll see you out on the drill yard in five minutes. And remember: this would not be a good day to be late. You need to start impressing us, and believe me we're not impressed yet. So if you don't want this to be the longest day of your lives, get moving. NOW!'

Without thinking, I followed the boys as they hurtled towards the men's changing room. What else was I supposed to do? Nobody had mentioned an alternative, and hadn't we just been told it didn't matter what sex we were any more? Judging by the terrified looks on the boys' faces, the last thing on their mind was seeing a girl undress in front of them. Thankfully, a makeshift physical barrier had been erected using some metal lockers, and I ducked behind it to change. Within seconds, I'd stripped down to my bra and knickers and put on my drill kit.

In a daze, I dashed out into the summer sunshine.

★   ★   ★

It was the running I hated the most. Every morning, after roll call and dress inspection, we would set off on a 3.5-mile circuit through the local fields. I'd always hated cross-country at school, and this — combined with the sweltering midsummer heat — made it a living hell. And that was before you factored in the boys' dismissive attitude towards me. Of all of them, I'd quickly figured out that Matthew Caston was the least happy about me being there. Tall, dark-haired and with a permanent sneer whenever I was around, in a previous life he'd clearly been a fly I'd splattered on the windscreen. 'Eat my dust, Reynolds!' he would shout scornfully as he barged past me each day, laughing with the others as he raced off into the distance. 'See you in a couple of hours.'

To make matters worse, on arrival back in the drill yard Eddie Zipfel would usually be standing there with an impish grin on his face. 'Congratulations, recruits ... you've completed the course,' he would say, completely deadpan. 'However, I know you can do better. Much better. So as a special treat, you're going to do it all again. Starting now. Off you go . . . ' This meant that most mornings we would run a total of *seven* bloody miles. I calculated that each painful pace took me two feet forwards, leaving me only another 18,478 to complete as I set out each morning. Even now, if I close my eyes I can still recall the mental checklist I used to help me through this daily torture: turn right at the wooden shed; cross the railway bridge past the sad-looking donkey; turn left behind the industrial estate; then run along the main road until you reach the gap in the hedge. And whatever happens, I told myself, do not, I repeat, do not throw up.

When I finally stumbled down the bank onto the gravel drill yard I was invariably sweaty, gasping for breath and ghostly pale. 'Ah, very good of you to join us at last, Firefighter Reynolds!' Eddie would say as I fell into line next to the boys, who needless to say had all finished the course at least fifteen minutes before me. Then, and only then, would our day begin.

* * *

Our first four weeks were given over to what was called 'Basic Training'. Which is exactly what it was. It was finally time to learn what exactly the job entailed, from the bottom up. This was the point where our instructors — Leading Fireman Paul Holmes and Sub Officer Eddie Zipfel — came into their own. Like a cross between Little and Large and the archetypal good cop, bad cop, they were a natural double act.

Baby-faced and easygoing, Paul Holmes was in charge of the day-to-day running of the course. He acted as a mentor we could always turn to if we were unhappy about anything. Eddie Zipfel on the other hand, while more senior in rank, took the bad-cop role. I would later discover that he was a born comedian who would leave me in fits of laughter, but for now, he was the authority figure who would dream up elaborate punishments when we made mistakes or started to get complacent.

'Right, now I know that your current knowledge of fire service procedures could be written on the back of a postage stamp,' said Paul, staring directly at me (and with good reason, I might add). 'Now, however, is when you get to learn about the tools of the trade. These are the things you will need to save other people's lives and which just might save your own. So pay very close attention . . . '

* * *

In our first week we learned how to run out the 25-metre lengths of standard Angus Duraline hose, how to link these lengths together and how to put a nozzle into one end, which firemen call a branch. If it sounds simple, believe me it wasn't. Because the truth about hose running was that it could be brutal. The Duraline would rub the skin off my poor knuckles and as my arms grew tired the heavy loops would start to drop and fall like giant rolls of out-of-control spaghetti.

There were also endless hose relays to look forward to. These would involve running out a 25-metre length of hose before dropping to one knee and extending my left arm for the hose to be picked up like a baton. If the guy behind me got it wrong, which he invariably did, I would feel the full force of the heavy metal coupling at the end of his hose whacking me in the back of the head or neck.

Then there were the day-to-day duties. We learned how to put a standpipe onto a water hydrant, how ropes (which, confusingly, were called lines) were used and how they had to be stored in a specific way in canvas bags to ensure they didn't get tangled. Even this seemingly simple task was treated with the solemnity of an ancient Japanese art form.

Each line would have one end dropped into the bottom of its own specific and identified canvas bag, then passed hand over hand to ensure that there were never any knots. Every bag was designed for a different length of line, and this careful stowing meant that each one could quickly be put into action in an emergency.

Most of these procedures were borrowed from the Royal Navy, and we also learned how to march, salute and respond to every order with a brisk 'Yes, sir!' Had I joined the army? Well, at least my old careers advisor Miss Jones would approve, I thought to myself as we stomped endlessly around the parade ground.

We also learned that anything and everything we touched needed to be spotless. 'That's still dirty, guys,' Paul or Eddie would say, staring at a gleaming hub-cap we had spent the last hour polishing. 'Do it again.' Daily duties included blasting behind the wheel arches of the fire engine with a high-pressure hose, shining the tyres with black boot polish and rubbing dirt from the windscreen with a chamois leather until it gleamed. On top of that, every flat surface had to be swept daily with stiff-bristle yard brooms, and the drill yard had to be constantly weeded and pruned until it looked fit for the Chelsea Flower Show.

In the second week things moved up a gear.

It was time to learn about the Bedford fire engine itself — now known simply as 'the pump', or 'the appliance'. This, it turned out, had more secret compartments than a magician's box. Each of its lockers contained more firefighting equipment, and we learned how to find each one, put it together and make it work. As we did so, Paul and Eddie would constantly shoot questions at us, forcing us to absorb the stream of information rather than let it drift over us. Where were the four lengths of suction hose stowed? How did the high-pressure hose reel work? What did it mean to put the 'pump in gear'? How did you unfasten the light portable pump?

Rather than use plain English — which would clearly be much too straightforward — our instructions were delivered using Navy jargon. 'Prepare to slip, slip, under-run, prepare to extend, extend, trip, head in/out, head left/right, heel out' became commands we learned to understand and act upon without a second thought.

And then there were the ladders — always the ladders. Who could have imagined there would be so many, and in so many different sizes? Like the fire service's answer to twitchers, we learned to spot the difference between the lesser-spotted wooden Ajax, the

Bailey 10.5-metre single extension and the 13.5-metre alloy double extension at a moment's notice.

In case that wasn't enough, there was also a three-piece short extension ladder, which we stripped down to create a triangular dam with lines and salvage sheets. Every one of them, we discovered, had multiple uses, designed to manage any and every possible scenario. And on it went. We would then be told to re-stow the equipment as fast as we had rolled it out, before a debriefing that would usually end up with us being asked to do it all again. Except faster. We went over these basic details until the answers were drummed into our heads; then, and only then, would the more complex drills begin.

By far the worst of these involved the Coventry Climax light portable pump, which was used to draw water on 'shouts' (call-outs) where a water hydrant wasn't an option. There was even a poster of the wretched thing on the wall of the classroom — where any normal workplace might have had, say, a Pirelli calendar — and I quickly learned this must be some kind of sick joke. Essentially, a 300-kilogram car engine with a large pump attached, it took four of us to carry it down to the river to start on the day's drill. Lifting it back up the hill afterwards, my heart would be beating like a jackhammer, which at least took my mind off the blisters.

Alongside these physical tests came a crash-course in how they all worked. I was fascinated to discover that situated in the belly of the fire engine was a water tank containing 400 gallons of water. This made it quite a weapon, and if they were in a playful mood, Paul and Eddie would ask us to attach multiple rolls of 25-metre hose together, all while it was still charged with water, making the hose ridiculously long. 'Firefighter Reynolds, take control of the situation!' Eddie would shout as my fellow recruits sniggered with amusement. This would be my cue to 'ride the snake'. This involved leaping on top of the hose at the end furthest away from the branch as it thrashed and slithered across the parade ground like a crazed anaconda. I would then have to crawl along it, using my whole body weight to wrestle the hose under control. Once I'd finally made it to the end — with water spurting everywhere — I would have to use any remaining energy to turn off the water supply at the hose's nozzle before collapsing in a soaking wet heap. 'Well done, Reynolds, we'll make a firefighter of you yet!' Eddie would say as I returned to my place on the drill line, sopping wet and muttering under my breath.

The relentless nature of these activities meant that almost every day I would throw up; either in a ditch during our morning run, or on the drill yard. This was considered mandatory: no one batted an eyelid if I or one of the boys took a minute to double over and do what we had to. 'If you're not feeling sick then you're not working hard enough,' would be Paul or Eddie's only comment as I resumed the drill, still feeling nauseous.

Every day I'd sweat so much my t-shirt would be drenched, my legs would feel like lead weights and my arms would ache so much I thought they'd drop off. But I still couldn't wait to get back there the next morning. Carving up wrecked cars using Cengar saws and zip guns, racing up 10.5-metre ladders, the occasional water fight — you don't see a lot of that working nine to five!

Paul and Eddie, meanwhile, managed to walk the tightrope between pushing us as hard as they could while acknowledging that we weren't screwing up completely. While we only ever addressed them as 'LF' (Paul) or 'Sub' (Eddie), they did their best to inject some humour into proceedings. Punishment drills would often come with the instruction 'Push-ups forever — begin!' and the sense that we were being transformed from kids off the street into responsible members of society felt like nothing I'd ever experienced before.

At lunchtime, rather than be left to our own devices, we'd be driven over to the brigade headquarters at Whitegates. Here, we'd sit alongside working firemen and dream of the day when we would be treated as equals as we tucked into huge platefuls of cottage pie with all the trimmings, followed by sponge pudding and custard. This would set us up nicely for soporific afternoons in the classroom with our heads buried in our red fire service manuals. Here we'd learn about the effect heat had on different construction materials, and I'd will the clock to reach five o'clock when we would be dismissed.

As I filed out of the building on my second Friday, I saw Eddie standing by the exterior door leading out onto the drill yard. Each day, he and Paul would dismiss the class formally, after which the others would watch as I went through my daily ritual of trying to start the bashed-up red Avenger I'd bought with my savings from waitressing. This involved perching my bum on the edge of the bonnet and bouncing it up and down until there was a loud clicking sound, triggering the starter motor. On a bad day, it could take ten minutes and my efforts were the cause of much hilarity among the boys, who never offered to help. This time as I left, Eddie gave me a conspiratorial wink. It was exactly what I needed. Aside from my chronically slow pace at the cross-country run, I thought I'd been doing OK, and this confirmed it. My spirits soared. No longer was I plain little Jo, a slightly scatty seventeen-year-old with no clear direction in life. I was a trainee firefighter.

After a couple of weeks of complete abstinence from alcohol, it was time to let my hair down. 'Right, get your glad rags on, we're going out,' I said to Graeme when I arrived home, finding him, as usual, holed up in his room, playing records. 'I'm a working girl now and I'm taking you out for a meal.'

Half an hour later, sitting at a corner table in the local Pizza Hut, I felt proud of what I'd already achieved. 'So, it seems you're really going to make a go of this firefighting lark,' said Graeme, carefully removing the anchovies from his Marinara pizza. 'Soon, you won't want to go to noisy punk gigs with me any more. You'll be wanting to hang out with your new macho men buddies instead.' There was a pause. Was he joking? Of course he was. We'd been hanging out together for six months and I'd reached that point where I knew every inflection of his voice, every wry look, every signal, no matter how understated. But I played along, just for the hell of it.

'Don't be daft,' I replied. 'It's just a job. But come to think of it, some of them *are* pretty good-looking.'

'It sounds like a right laugh,' he continued, refusing to rise to the bait. 'I mean, what other occupation allows you to have water fights and get paid for it? And there I was thinking they were going to make your life hell.'

We didn't say anything more about it, and I was so hungry after my exertions, all I could really think about was getting as much value as I could from the 'all you can eat' salad bar. But there was one black cloud on the horizon I didn't mention. From our very first day I'd heard talk about an instructor who specialized in putting the fear of God into new recruits. His name was Assistant Divisional Officer Gallagher and we would be meeting him the next week. As I munched on a well-earned pizza, however, I put the thought out of my mind. I'd worry about Gallagher on Monday.

4

Under Pressure

'He's here,' whispered Ray Harcourt to me, as we took up our seats in the classroom on the Monday morning after our daily run. 'Who's here?' I asked innocently, as I noticed both Paul and Eddie's faces tense slightly as a swarthy figure in full dress uniform stepped out of the red Austin Ambassador that had just pulled up in the fire-station car park. 'What do you mean, who's here?' Ray hissed, a bead of sweat breaking out on his forehead. 'Gallagher of course!'

So, I thought, he really does exist. For the last fortnight I had heard constant references to 'ADO Gallagher', 'Gallagher' or simply 'that mad bastard Gallagher' from all quarters. This was a man, legend had it, who liked nothing better than making the lives of trainee firefighters a complete and utter misery.

'I've heard that he made one trainee lick the entire drill yard clean after he'd caught him carrying a line bag with his teeth,' a quivering Neil Dallas had told me one day over lunch. 'He'd said, 'I've got no fucking idea where your tongue has been, so maybe it will teach you to treat your kit with a bit more respect.' I've also heard he made one recruit carry hoses around the drill until the metal lugs cut into his neck so much he almost died from bleeding.'

I took these stories with a pinch of salt, as well as the rumours that Gallagher's 'beasting' of new recruits reached Olympic standards of savagery. Surely, I thought to myself, nothing as prehistoric as that can still go on in progressive and enlightened 1982, can it?

Then I saw him. Shaven-headed, and scarily tall in his highly glossed regimental boots, ADO Gallagher seemed larger than nature intended. If the razor-sharp creases in his uniform told you he was a stickler for detail, the way the chinstrap of his regimental cap was perched on the point of his chin told you that he was a showman, too. If the whole world was a stage, then the drill yard at Wymondham was where he always had the starring role.

In a few brief seconds the *crunch-crunch-crunch* of his boots on the gravel outside was followed by the opening of our classroom door. Authority crackled around Gallagher like a force-field, and as he stood in front of us I desperately avoided eye contact. Like a fly trapped in a spider's web, I sat at my desk unable to move, knowing that my only hope was that death would come quickly and painlessly.

He had noticed me immediately, and with one giant stride came and stood directly in front of me, squatting down and leaning forwards, giving me no option but to look directly into his eyes. Two black pits of nothingness, they looked at me in the indifferent way a shark's might do. *Feeding time*, they seemed to say. Just as I was bracing myself for the worst day of my life, however, the storm passed as quickly as it had arrived. 'That will be all,' he said, rising back up to his full height and striding out of the classroom as quickly as he'd arrived.

This introduction into ADO Gallagher's way of doing things set a pattern. It was uncanny. One minute we could be in the classroom, happily working through one of the exercises Paul and Eddie had devised for us. The next, the temperature would suddenly dip a couple of degrees as his red Austin Ambassador pulled up in the car park. This would be followed by him beckoning for us to join him on the drill yard, effectively calling a halt to the programme Paul and Eddie had devised for the day.

'Right, ladies, you don't seem to have any idea of why you're here,' he'd begin, after we'd nervously shuffled out to where he was standing. 'I want you lot to impress me. Or at least give me some reason for hope. It's time for you to show me why we shouldn't shut this course down. So get moving!'

No matter how simple the drill, sheer terror on one of our parts would result in an error that drew the full weight of Gallagher's wrath. Hotter than a blast furnace, his paint-stripping barrage of abuse was delivered at the kind of ear-splitting volume I'd only ever heard used by Sergeant-Major Williams on *It Ain't Half Hot Mum*. Except nobody was laughing here. 'How effin' stupid can one woman be, Firefighter Reynolds?' he'd holler inches from my face after I'd failed to connect two hoses properly. 'I've seen ballet dancers with more strength than you. I've seen old ladies out walking on the common who move faster than you. I've seen effin' chimpanzees with more intelligence than you. Why on earth should I be wasting my time teaching you to do these things if you won't ever bloody learn?'

'I'm doing my best, ADO Gallagher,' I'd hear myself say, desperately attempting to maintain some dignity, as the peak of his regimental cap pressed into my forehead.

'Well, right now, Firefighter Reynolds, your best just isn't good enough,' he'd respond, before singling out one of the others for some other minor error. Anyone questioning his authority was either clinically insane or harbouring a death wish, and like the creature from the Black Lagoon he even managed to instil fear in his absence. 'I've heard Gallagher's coming this afternoon,' someone would whisper in the canteen at lunchtime, and the ravenous appetite I'd worked up would be replaced by a sickening feeling in the pit of my stomach. Even more chilling would be the times when he barely said anything, speaking so quietly it was even more dreadful than the full-on earbashing.

It was in my fourth week that I began to worry that I might not make the grade. The emphasis throughout our month-long induction course had been on building our upper body strength, and I could tell that I was lagging some way behind the others purely because I hadn't yet built enough muscle. On the Monday of our fourth week, Gallagher appeared on the drill yard unexpectedly and, without saying anything to the others, asked me to follow him into Paul Holmes's office. My heart was pounding and I sensed that my marching orders might be coming a week early. Closing the door behind him and shutting all the blinds, he sat behind the desk, leaned back in the chair and looked me over like a sunbathing crocodile.

'Trainee Reynolds — why are you here?' he said, his voice barely above a whisper. What did he mean? Had I made some cardinal error? Or was he referring to my being in the fire service, which I was pretty sure he disapproved of?

'Because I'm training to become a firefighter, sir.' A pause. One that felt like time had stood still.

'I know that,' he continued, appraising every inch of my trembling physique. 'What I'm asking you is, do you really think you've got the upper body strength to achieve that aim, Reynolds?'

I knew I had to fight my corner. If I didn't, Gallagher was well within his rights to recommend that I neither had the physical nor mental strength to carry out the job I'd signed up for. I pushed my shoulders back and looked him straight in the eye.

'I believe I will have, sir, if I'm given the chance.'

Silence. All-pervasive, nerve-shredding, knee-knocking silence.

Should I say something else? Maybe not. His body language suggested he was mulling this answer over and shouldn't be further provoked. My future was in his hands, and as I stood there, I felt as if my life had been put on pause. What on earth was he waiting for? Finally, he spoke.

'Give me fifty press-ups, Reynolds, right now.'

Was he kidding? Probably not. Which meant this must be a test. Or was he just trying to find a way of forcing me out? Don't ask me how I managed it, but five minutes later the ordeal was over. I'd completed the task, and there even seemed to be a twinkle of amusement in his eyes as I got to my feet.

'You're dismissed, Reynolds. Go back and join the rest of the recruits on the drill yard.'

As I pulled up outside my dad's house that evening and turned off the ignition, I took one final drag of my roll-up and looked at my reflection in the rearview mirror. Things will get better, I said silently to myself, as I put my key in the door and greeted everyone with my customary broad smile. They had to.

★ ★ ★

'A-ha! Here she is, Norfolk's answer to Wonder Woman!' said Graeme, handing me a mug of tea and a slice of Bakewell tart as I slumped in front of the TV. No one looked up. BBC *Look East* had just finished and the weather forecast was on. For some reason this was seen as the evening's TV highlight. 'It's going to be cloudy tomorrow,' said my dad.

It was a Monday, I had just got home after another long day at work, and it wasn't just my regulation black socks that were making me feel uncomfortable. As the weeks went by, it was becoming increasingly clear to me that the fire service and I had what a divorce lawyer might call 'irreconcilable differences'. My heroines were Siouxsie Sioux, Chrissie Hynde and Annie Lennox, and seeing them project a powerful, entirely feminine strength on *Top of the Pops* every Thursday only made me want to assert my individuality more. Yet the fire service was all about subsuming my personal identity and taking on a strictly defined role. On the rare nights when I wasn't out on the town with Graeme, I would retreat upstairs to my tiny attic room and indulge in my own — very minor — act of rebellion. Fire service regulations stipulated that no makeup or nail polish should ever be worn on duty. However, I always ensured my toenails were immaculately painted fire-engine red. It was the last vestige of femininity available to me, and I hung on to it like a life raft.

My additional X chromosome was causing problems in other ways, too. Rather than bonding with my new workmates, I felt isolated. It wasn't their fault, it was just that as the only woman firefighter at Wymondham, or anywhere in the Norfolk Fire Service, I would always be the odd one out. I felt an invisible barrier of loneliness engulfing me. On good days, I convinced myself I was an undercover agent in the male workplace. But I quickly discovered that men don't talk to each other the way women do. In fact, in my experience, they will talk about anything *but* how they feel. This was made blindingly clear to me every morning at roll call. Arriving at 8.45 a.m. sharp, I would sit in silence as the boys chewed over the pressing issues of the day; whether Samantha Fox or Linda Lusardi had the most impressive 'bazookas', or the thrilling details from the latest Motocross championship.

On one level, this testosterone-charged chit-chat was completely understandable. These boys had signed up for the most macho profession going, and the last thing they needed was a girl on the course cramping their style. But it didn't stop me feeling that I wouldn't mind too much if the earth swallowed me up.

On top of that, the physical challenges put in front of me were daunting — literally so in the case of the training tower. A four-storey brick drill tower in one corner of the drill yard with balconies and stairwells, it was designed to resemble an inner-city tower block. Some mornings, even the sight of it made me feel queasy, and I dreaded the moment when we would start using it. The usual scenario would go something like this. To pitch the ladder against the base of the tower, on a command of 'Squad, squad 'shun — prepare to slip, slip!', four of us would remove the 13.5-metre aluminium ladder from the top of the pump and run towards the tower.

Having reached the base of the tower, we would then balance the ladder vertically, pointing straight to the heavens, while the other two 'footed' it at the base. It was only on the order 'Prepare to extend — extend!' that the head of the ladder was laid against the brick-face of the tower. After a final barked instruction of 'Trip, head in/out, head left/right, heel out!', one by one we would run up it in search of a body that had been hidden somewhere inside. This 'body' would be in the form of my old friend the sand dummy, which once located would be brought back down using a classic 'firemen's lift', which meant descending the ladder blind. All the while, Paul and Eddie would be urging us on, shouting 'Faster, Faster!' as we attempted to beat our previous record time. If any of the six of us made a mistake, we would have to do the whole drill again. Only quicker.

Each gruelling test would end with me covered in small cuts and random bruises, and after a while it felt like even the hose was out to get me. While I enjoyed learning how to hold it properly, gripping it tightly between my right arm and my body, the constant unreeling and re-stowing of the hoses meant I was always bashing my knees or cutting my hands on the sharp heavy metal lugs. I knew I could never let on how much pain I was in, but the truth was that despite my height and agility, I simply didn't have the physical strength of the boys.

This sense of exclusion became more acute on our day trips away from Wymondham to learn different aspects of the job. Once a week we would travel to Norwich City Technical College where we would listen to fascinating lectures about the molecular structure of a brick. For the first few weeks we had to do this in full uniform, which instantly set us apart from our fellow students, who looked down on us as some lower form of life. As a consequence, I quickly realized that the chances of making any new friends there were a big fat zero.

Rather than be the proverbial gooseberry as the rest of class huddled in various cliques during breaks, I would sit alone upstairs in the canteen, gazing out of the window as I ate my pre-packed cheese roll and wondering if I'd made a terrible mistake.

This sense of impending doom only got worse when we started on our lifesaving proficiency badges. I was such a weak swimmer I got scared in the bath, and our trips to St Augustine's swimming pool in Norwich every Thursday filled me with dread. This decrepit Victorian public baths was so awash with chlorine my eyes and nostrils would sting for days after each visit, and I'd change into my modest navy blue swimsuit in a cold, damp cubicle while wishing I was anywhere else. This weekly torture was overseen by an instructor called Nicky Excel. Built like an Olympic swimming champion, but with a voice like a braying horse, he seemed convinced that he should have been a stand-up comedian. 'Morning, laydeeez!' he would wheeze at the start of each session. 'Whose bed did we get out the wrong side of this morning?'

As I plunged into the icy green pool, I truly felt in at the deep end. The weeks stretched out ahead of me, tempting me to fail. How could I possibly make it through? I felt an urgent need to tell someone about how I was feeling. Seeing as I never spoke to my mum and dad seriously about anything, there was only one alternative.

★　★　★

'He said what?' said Graeme, standing over the stove as eight rashers of Danepak sizzled in the frying pan. It was Saturday morning, the sun was shining and we were about to enjoy our weekend tradition of bacon sarnies drowning in Heinz tomato ketchup. I should have been full of my usual high spirits. But the fact was, I felt utterly miserable. While most of my friends from Whitland were heading off for exciting new lives at university, my days were spent lugging hoses and heavy machinery across what was, basically, a car park. While other girls my age dreamed about snogging Adam Ant or Paul Weller, my fantasies revolved around ADO Gallagher contracting a terrible disease that would prevent him from ever reporting for duty at Wymondham again.

'Graeme . . . I really don't know how I can carry on,' I blurted out, not being able to hold back my tears as he placed the sandwich on the kitchen table in front of me. 'I'm the only girl there and all they ever talk about is

63

how 'you're only as strong as the weakest link in the chain'. I can tell they all think that's me. It would be easier for everyone if I quit.'

'Come on, Jo,' he said, in a tone he reserved for matters of the gravest importance. 'Most of the time you come back here bouncing off the walls with excitement. You've said it countless times — the fire service is the best thing that ever happened to you.'

I had a slurp of hot black coffee and pondered. Maybe he was right. I knew the job was making me fitter, testing my limits and teaching me new skills. I just couldn't help feeling that it was also taking a terrible toll on my self-esteem. I was losing the identity I'd fought so hard for by leaving home at sixteen. 'I just feel like I'm becoming a cog in a machine.'

'Listen, we're all cogs in the machine one way or the other — look at me,' he said, as a dollop of ketchup oozed from his sandwich and landed on his most prized Ramones t-shirt. 'The thing to remember is that once you've qualified you'll be with people who respect you for having done the hard yards. You've just got to get through this stage. From that point on, you'll be a firefighter. And everyone loves a firefighter. Even me. And I'm a hardcore punk rocker.'

With the words 'Have this — it might cheer you up,' he handed me a little tin badge, painted with the slogan 'Different Day, Same Shit'. I vowed to treasure this lucky talisman and keep it safely on me at all times. If things got too much, I'd have something to keep me sane. 'But listen,' he added, suddenly serious, 'you've got to tell them how you feel. It's new for them, too, remember. They probably don't know if they're being too hard or too soft on you either. How are they going to know unless you tell them?'

★   ★   ★

As I lurched from lamppost to lamppost the following Monday on our daily run, I saw Paul Holmes trotting up behind me. It was time to take the bull by the horns. The boys had run off in the distance, and there was no one else about other than me, and Paul.

'Listen, LF, I really don't know how long I'm going to be able to put up with this,' I said when he caught up with me. 'Let's face it, I'm a fish out of water here. There are no facilities for me; I'm wearing a man's uniform; the rest of the boys act like I don't exist. It's also pretty obvious from the attitude of ADO Gallagher that I'm not wanted round here.'

Paul gave me a look that I would come to be very familiar with. 'Well, Jo, I'll level with you,' he said, having made sure the others were out of earshot. 'We're all on new ground here. This whole course is an experiment. As you know, most firemen only train for three months, so there's lots of opposition to this course from the top brass. They say it's a waste of time and resources to train you lot for so long. However, I've seen nothing that tells me you won't be able to pass with flying colours and prove the whole blinkin' lot of them wrong. In fact, on a lot of levels, you're a great recruit. I shouldn't say this, but you bring a lot to the team.' Was he really talking about me? 'So don't you dare give up, you hear me?' he continued, grinning as he nudged me in the ribs. 'If I've learned anything about you over the past few weeks, Jo Reynolds, it's that you're not a quitter. You might be having a dark time, but you'll get through it. Then imagine how great it will be when you do get to pass out. Which you will. It's our job to make sure you do, remember?'

Whether this was the truth or just an expertly delivered bit of kidology, I'll never know, but it certainly lifted my spirits on that hazy day in September 1982.

5

We Are Family

As my confidence grew and the months rolled by, I began to realize that there was one of the boys — Neil Dallas — with whom I actually had something in common. We both loved music and had gradually become friends, swapping notes most lunchtimes in the mess room at Whitegates about the bands we'd heard on John Peel's show the previous night. Compared to the manly banter surrounding us, it must have sounded pretty strange. 'Did you hear the new Pigbag single?' I'd enthuse. 'Yeah — amazing. And what about the one by It's Immaterial, 'A Gigantic Raft in the Philippines'?'

Neil was crazy about a synth-pop outfit called A Flock of Seagulls, and drove everyone mad by singing one of their tunes, 'It's Not Me Talking', at any opportunity.

'Keep quiet at the back there, Dallas!' Paul or Eddie would say, on catching him chatting away to me during a lengthy exposition on how to coil a line correctly.

'Sorry, sir!' he would respond, flashing me

a grin, before following up with a hummed rendition of 'It's Not Me Talking'.

As well as getting on with Neil, I also discovered that — hurrah! — there were parts of the job I actually enjoyed. When our red fire service manuals were turned to the section entitled 'Knots', I suddenly felt my anxieties vanish. As we learned how to tie and untie every knot known to man I found the need for lateral thinking suited me perfectly.

Our ability — or lack of it — to complete the half-hitch knot, the round-turn, the two-half hitches and the bowline was tested constantly, and when we could tie, untie and recognize each knot perfectly we were blindfolded and made to tie them again. My natural aptitude for solving puzzles meant that I could complete all these tasks faster than anyone else in the class. At last, something I was good at!

As I got fitter, drills that at first had seemed impossible also suddenly seemed easy — even the ones involving the dreaded Training Tower. Equally, as the drills became more complex, they became more about thinking on your feet than brute strength. To ensure they were as realistic as possible, these would always be sprung on us at a moment's notice. One minute we could be half asleep in the classroom, watching flies buzzing against the windows as we worked through the fire service manual, the next we would be attending a mocked-up RTA (road traffic accident) in the drill yard. 'Right, you lot, there's a car on fire, with a heavily pregnant woman trapped inside it. Move!' Paul would bark as we flew into action. As we set about controlling the situation he would add in elements as it suited him. 'The petrol tank is leaking, her leg is broken and she's becoming unconscious.'

To add realism, Eddie would play the role of an incapacitated driver, covered in fake blood and screaming in agony at every attempt to move him. These were the situations I enjoyed the most. We had some amazing specialized rescue equipment at our disposal, and I loved getting to grips with the high-pressure 'Jaws of Life' in practice rescues, and even the more modest Cengar saw, which was essentially only an air-saw with a hack-blade in it. We spent a lot of time using this rescue equipment in ingenious ways, taking the doors off a car wreck, cutting metal pillars, and, best of all, triumphantly lifting off the whole of a car roof to access the casualty.

I also loved applying first aid and would happily take up this role at any incident, assessing the damage and ensuring the victim was receiving the Entonox gas — equal amounts of nitrous oxide and oxygen — which acted as an analgesic.

I especially loved engaging with the victim on an emotional level, and being the voice of calm and reassurance. In a typical RTA the injured party would have been in the car up to fifteen minutes before we got there. If they were still alive, they would have been through the worst shock imaginable, and may have been trapped in a vehicle that, if the petrol tank had been damaged, could ignite at any second. The best way to deal with the shock was to make an instant personal connection. 'Hello darling, what's your name?' I'd enquire, regardless of whether we were supposed to be dealing with a man, woman or child. 'Don't worry, we're here now, and we're going to do everything we can to take care of you.'

I learned that the important thing was never to make any promises about how long it would take to get them out, but to keep them engaged and, most important of all, conscious. To lighten the mood, every now and then Eddie would scream out in horror something like 'Hang on a minute! You're not a fireman, you're a woman! What are you doing here?' making me explain that yes, indeed I was a woman, but I was also a trained firefighter.

We were learning how to work as part of a team, and the initial reservations I'd had about the boys started to melt away. We each had unique characteristics we brought to any task, and, after a good day on the drill yard, would share the warm glow that comes from a job done well. Having a car was also helping me make friends, and I'd regularly give one or other of them a lift as I drove home to Norwich each day.

As we packed up the kit for the umpteenth time one afternoon, I found myself walking beside one of the other boys, Ray. I didn't connect with him in the same way as Neil, but he never had any airs and graces, and we got on well enough. 'I appreciate that this is all good practice,' he said, out of Paul and Eddie's earshot. 'But I can't wait to get out of here and do it for real. At this rate, it feels like we'll never see an RTA outside of Wymondham.'

I was too exhausted to talk, and grunted agreement. But like they say: be careful what you wish for. Little did we know it as we re-stowed the hoses and packed the gear away, our own personal tragedy was just around the corner.

★　★　★

It had been another long afternoon in the classroom solving knotty problems, and I was losing the will to live. We'd spent the past four months slaving our guts out on the drill yard, lifting ladders, connecting hoses and scrubbing everything that moved, and I felt like we needed a break. Thankfully, so did Paul and Eddie. 'Right, recruits . . . seeing as you've applied yourself well over the last sixteen weeks, we think it's time you had a small reward,' explained Paul as we were packing away. 'No, it's not two weeks in Marbella. But it is a change of scenery. You'll be spending the next week at Easton Agricultural College.' I could hear he was still talking, but already my mind was racing ahead. At last! A week away from the bloody drill yard and Gallagher. Seven days without strapping on my plastic yellow waders and lugging the Coventry Climax down to the river and back. Life couldn't get much better. 'Not only will you find out about what goes on at the neighbouring farms, you'll be expected to muck in and make yourself useful. Is that perfectly clear?' Crystal, I thought to myself. Who knows? It might even be fun?

By 9.30 a.m. on our first day I realized that, much like everything else in the fire service, our week away was going to be bloody hard work. Most of it was spent on

72

barn cleaning duties. This involved sweeping countless dusty, cobweb-filled haylofts the size of aircraft hangars with wooden brooms. A task that, by my reckoning, would take us until Doomsday. 'Well, this is going to be a laugh,' said Neil sarcastically, as we entered a huge hayloft that looked like it hadn't been cleaned for a decade. The next thing I knew, he was striding across the barn, broom under his arm like a regimental cane. 'My name is Assistant Divisional Officer Gallagher,' he bellowed in an uncanny impersonation of our favourite drill instructor. 'My navel is central. My conscience is clear. My will is with my solicitors, Short & Curly. That is all you need to know about me. You are here to sweep, and sweep is what you are bloody well going to do.'

With Neil around, the entertainment never stopped. When he wasn't cracking daft jokes or pulling faces, he'd entertain me by balancing the tip of his broom in the dimple on his chin, staggering around like Tommy Cooper in an effort to keep it vertical, all the while singing 'It's Not Me Talking'. It was if he knew the punchline to some cosmic joke most people weren't even aware existed, and he made what could have been the dullest week of my life one of the funniest.

Back at Wymondham, we were about to

head off home one afternoon when Neil mentioned that he was going to get a lift home on the back of Matthew Caston's motorbike. Matthew and I had never seen eye to eye, and his habit of screeching to a halt in the car park on his flashy 750cc Yamaha always put my teeth on edge. If you want to cadge a lift home with Norfolk's answer to Evel Knievel, I thought to myself, that's fine by me. Besides, I was already running my own unpaid taxi service, and that night I was dropping both Ray and Stewart Graveling off in my trusty Avenger as I made my return trip to Eastern Road.

It had been a constructive day, and spirits were high as the three of us jokily sang along to Abba's 'Dancing Queen' on the radio and swapped gossip about Wymondham and its curious ways. Usually, Matthew would roar off into the traffic, never to be seen again, but I noticed that he'd been caught up in a jam and when we were halfway home I noticed he was directly in front of us, impatiently trying to thread his way past the delivery lorries making their way into the city centre.

It all happened in an instant. Seeing a momentary gap in the traffic, Matthew had pulled out to overtake, but veered back in sharply when he saw a car coming the other way. Too late. He'd lost control of the bike as he swerved and I watched in horror as it veered straight into the path of an oncoming car.

Time froze. Was this happening? As if in suspended animation, I watched the ash falling from my cigarette, heard 'Dancing Queen' slow to 33rpm, and saw my own pupils dilate in the rearview mirror.

A sickening thud jolted me back to my senses. In a flash, Ray had jumped out of the passenger seat and sprinted towards the tangled mess on the road in front of us. I tried to concentrate, putting on my hand-brake and hazard lights to avoid another accident. But in the time I'd done that, Ray was back at the car. He'd been gone thirty seconds, but he'd aged ten years. 'It's Neil,' he said flatly, all blood drained from his face. No! No, please don't say that, it can't be. I felt the world stop. But I also knew I couldn't just sit there. I needed to do something. Anything. With my legs like jelly, I jumped out of the car. 'You go and see what you can do, and I'll go and get help,' I said, conscious that, by a twist of fate, we were barely 100 metres from the brigade headquarters at Whitegates.

As I ran blindly towards the house, I could see men in fire service uniforms running towards me. They'd heard the collision and were rushing to help. As we reached the scene of the accident, it was clear that there was nothing any of us could do. Matthew had been thrown clear on impact, and was unharmed. But Neil had been killed instantly. It felt like the bitterest of ironies. After all the months of preparation we'd been through, our first emergency had been one we were involved in. And now one of us was dead.

A week later, there was a brigade funeral with full honours. Seeing so many of Norfolk's finest in full dress uniform brought everything into focus. Neil was still just a boy, and had been in the service only a few months, yet his passing was treated with the same solemnity which would have been afforded a heroic 'smoke-eater' of thirty-five years' standing. Finally, I was beginning to understand quite how magical and inclusive the world I'd entered into was. It was only in the pub afterwards that the sheer horror of what had happened overwhelmed me. I felt so awful for Neil's family, losing such a beautiful, bright soul. I felt confused. Broken. Words simply couldn't express it.

'It just seems such a terrible waste,' I said, when Eddie came over to me later as I was standing at the bar. Neil's family had left, and my brave face dissolved into a flood of tears. I couldn't understand how everyone could remain so stoical. 'I know you guys are really upset too. Why am I the only one who's bloody well crying?'

'It's a terrible thing that's happened, Jo,' he said, putting a reassuring arm around me. 'We're all hurting, too. But death is an occupational hazard in this job. Our job is to be there, clear up the mess and help people move on with their lives. It doesn't mean we don't care. The truth is, these guys care too much. They just don't tend to show it.'

Three weeks later, Matthew Caston returned to training. He'd come back early from compassionate leave, and I suppose he wanted to put the past behind him as much as we did. At the end of his first day back, Stuart Jeneson rushed out into the yard to have a word with him as Matthew clambered aboard his Yamaha and revved the throttle. Here we go, I thought, as the rest of us ran to the window to see how this mini-drama would play out. 'Hey Matthew, could you give me a lift home?' he said, and Eddie's words ran through my mind. We all exchanged glances, but no one said a word. They didn't have to. We were a family now. We'd get through this together. Although I thought about him every day, Neil's death was never mentioned again.

6

Sweet Dreams (Are Made of This)

At last, a place of my own. Even by my standards, I knew the room wasn't up to much. A large square-shaped box with grubby white walls and rotten window frames, it wasn't, I had to admit, The Ritz.

However, I had tried to make it as homely as possible. I'd covered the grimy-looking mattress left by the last tenants with a fetching beige bedspread, while the mis-matched curtains (thanks, Jean!) added, I thought, a bohemian feel. Once I'd artfully arranged my few possessions — a black bin liner of clothes, a Bush music centre and my two posters, one of Che Guevara, the other for The Sex Pistols' single 'God Save the Queen', the place looked rather stylish in my eyes.

This change of scenery had come about after Graeme casually mentioned at breakfast one morning that there was a room going spare in the house he was moving into with a couple of his musician friends. 'That sounds interesting, I might take you up on it,' I said, trying to sound nonchalant. Inside, my heart was beating like a steam-hammer. Boys! Guitars! My own front door key! What, exactly, was there not to like about the idea? 'OK, well, let me know, because the room's yours if you want it,' he mumbled, clearly unaware that I was mentally jumping cartwheels. *At last the fun can begin.*

Situated on the village green in nearby Pulham Market, The Laurels was a stone-built house dating back to the 1500s, and its high ceilings and broad oak beams reeked of history. However, I doubted even The Laurels had seen anything quite like it as its new occupants walked through its heavy oak front door one freezing cold morning in February 1983. As well as Graeme, my new house-mates were his best mate Adrian and girlfriend 'Ratty' Alison — so named because they never stopped arguing — and a swarthy musician called Mick they had met on the local pub circuit. They were left-leaning, army-surplus-wearing, dog-on-a-string types whose presence was guaranteed to get the neighbours' curtains twitching.

Best of all, from my perspective, none of them were remotely interested in the fire service or my role in it. I could have spent the last twelve hours dragging Tom Cruise, Terry Wogan and Angie from *EastEnders* from the burning set of *Blankety Blank*, and the response to my return home from work would still have been the same: 'All right, Jo. Put the kettle on, would you?'

After months of scrutiny, I couldn't wait to blend in with this new alternative crowd and see the world how they did. Most of the time, it must be said, this was through a cumulonimbus-sized cloud of spliff smoke. Much like on our favourite TV programme, *The Young Ones*, The Laurels was a place where everyday reality was kept at arm's length. When they weren't skinning up, the boys spent their time strumming their guitars or with their noses buried in stoner comics *The Fabulous Furry Freak Brothers* and *Fat Freddy's Cat*, issues of which were exchanged like holy sacraments. To add to the surreal mood, Graeme's pet budgerigar Claude was allowed to fly freely around the house, and would happily drink tea from any abandoned tea cup — that is, when he wasn't sitting on my shoulder and pecking at my earrings.

From my first afternoon there it was obvious that both Graeme and Adrian were in awe of Mick, who at the grand old age of twenty-four was treated as the fount of all knowledge. Mick drove a red GPO van with a mattress in the back. On the rear door a sticker read: 'If this van's a-rockin' don't bother knockin', and any admirers picked up after his gigs at local hotspot The Mischief Tavern would be treated to a night of passion in what he called his 'shag wagon'.

I'd never encountered such worldly sophistication before, and soon I too was under his spell. Most evenings after my nightly meal of fish fingers and mash — all I could afford on my £11-a-week wages — the five of us would huddle around the fire for warmth as Mick waxed lyrical on his favourite subject, the fly agaric mushroom. 'I'm telling you, they're out there,' he would babble like Richard Dreyfuss in *Close Encounters of the Third Kind*, as he described his journeys through Thetford Forest's 47,000 acres in search of the holy grail of psilocybin fungi. 'I've heard that there's some growing at the coast near Sheringham. I'm going out there next weekend.'.

Sure enough, each Saturday morning he would head out on his latest quest, the sound of the shag wagon backfiring as he set off acting as my weekend alarm call. Such dedication was contagious, and before long all four of us had decided to join him on a pilgrimage to the nearby woods at East Dereham, which Mick had declared 'the best magic mushroom fields in Norfolk'. Armed with a carrier bag each, we trudged through the fields with only the vaguest idea what we were looking for. Nonetheless, true to Mick's word, before long we had soon collected roughly a hundred mushrooms each. 'What do we do now?' I asked, as we examined the curious-looking fungi, standing in the car park. 'Well, eat them of course!' said Mick, throwing a large handful into his mouth and chewing vigorously. I glanced at Adrian and Graeme. Both of them were already wolfing down the raw mushrooms, and motioning for me to follow suit. How bad can it be? I thought, as I gulped down handful after handful, swigging Strongbow to take away the vile taste.

Our plan was then to drive to the car park on Castle Hill, which overlooked Norwich, before the driver's — in this case Graeme's — head exploded. None of us — not even Mick, the so-called 'expert' — knew that the 'recommended' dose was no more than thirty, and once they kicked in the results were terrifying. 'Oh my god, my hands are melting!' I whimpered, as, after half an hour of sitting in silence in the car park, horrible visions convinced me that I'd been transformed into a walking skeleton. One look on the grief-stricken faces of the others told me that they were all going through their own personal hells too.

'Look at that, a strawberry cheesecake!' said Graeme, staring intently at what even I could see was just one of these accursed fly agaric mushrooms. 'It's so beautiful, man, it's almost like it's . . . alive. I can see it . . . breathing.'

Up until this point I'd thought ADO Gallagher was scary, but seeing my friends mentally disintegrate in front of my eyes was a whole new level of horror. In a blind panic and desperate to make the visions stop, I desperately tried to roll a cigarette, dropping tobacco everywhere as my every move made me feel like I was staring into a kaleidoscope.

When we finally made it back to The Laurels about five hours later I retreated to the sanctuary of my room to sleep it off. As I lay in bed, staring up at my poster of Che Guevera, I could sense that my revolutionary hero was egging me on. Maybe I was about to reach a definitive conclusion about the meaning of life? Before I could reach it, however, I was violently sick. Then I passed out.

★ ★ ★

You know you're bored when your idea of fun is learning about fire extinguishers. But that was me, when Paul told us that we would be spending the next week doing precisely that at a company called U-K Wench.

To be honest, I wasn't that excited about it. But, hey, at least it counted as another week ticked off the training calendar. And whatever they had in store for us couldn't be as bad as running around those bloody fields!

It had been a quiet weekend at The Laurels, and as my trusty Avenger turned out of Pulham Market and towards Norwich rather than my usual commute to Wymondham, I felt pleased to have a break from the routine. Our mentor for the week was a guy called Tony Dickerson. A big, friendly sort, he had all the classic hallmarks of the ex-fireman: smartly dressed, highly polished shoes, and the kind of rock-solid eye contact that told you he was one of the good guys. Tony immediately made us feel comfortable, offering us tea and coffee and even — gasp — biscuits.

'First of all, I'm going to give you a tour of the factory,' he explained, once the custard creams had been put away. 'We have the proud record of making all the fire extinguishers in Norfolk, and we also provide fire protection to many different businesses in our area.'

The next week was spent learning about every type of fire extinguisher and how to use, service and even make them — it's amazing what you can do with a piece of sheet metal and some spray-paint. We even got a certificate to acknowledge our efforts, and I planned to take my shiny new red water fire extinguisher home to give to Dad to keep in his garage at Eastern Road.

However, if I thought that was going to be the end of the course, I was sorely mistaken. On the Friday afternoon, the five of us were driven from Tony's premises to Norwich airport, near to the village of Horsham St Faith. As we arrived and jumped out of the minibus, we were introduced to Chief Instructor Barry Harwood and Chris Carter. It was immediately obvious that there would be no more *Blue Peter*-style activities here.

'Recruits, get changed into your full firefighting kit, on the double!' ordered Harwood the minute our feet touched the ground. Once we were ready for action, we assembled at the far end of the runway tarmac, next to an aircraft graveyard crammed with ancient fuselages and aeronautical bric-a-brac. We then each pulled pieces of paper out of a hat to see which job we would have to do. Mine read 'FRONT'.

'OK, Reynolds, it looks like you've got the short straw — or the golden ticket, depending on which way you look at it,' said Harwood, explaining that my job was to be on the hose, with the responsibility of putting the blaze out. Just as I was taking this information in, Chris Carter's whole mood changed. There was suddenly a grave sense of urgency in his voice, and I realized the drill had already started.

'OK, junior firefighters, listen up. There is an emergency situation out on the airfield,' he said, pointing to the far side of the airport where plumes of smoke were visible. 'An aviation fuel tanker is on fire, and it will soon be out of control. We are counting on you to use speed and all of your combined skills to get it under control and extinguish it. Now move, there's not a second to waste!'

As we ran towards it, I tried to keep clear-headed, taking deep breaths as I felt my pulse racing in my ears. This was our first proper exercise without Paul and Ed's supervision, and smacked of a make-or-break test. The exercise situation had been set up in a part of the airfield where all the out-of-commission aeroplanes had been abandoned. Many of these surreal 'corpses' had random pieces cut out of their fuselages and as we weaved our way through them I could see a huge old dented fuel tanker billowing filthy black smoke. The oil had caught alight, and a fearsome-looking blaze was in progress. As I was in charge of the hose, it was down to me to take control of the situation. 'Guys, help me get some hoses out of this locker,' I said, pointing to the airport's pump, which had been positioned nearby. 'We need four lengths altogether, as quick as you can, with a branch on the end!'

The months of training were paying off — within seconds I was moving towards the blaze with Ray just behind me in support. As we got closer, a wave of heat from the dense, suffocating smoke hit me, and I started to sweat heavily. 'OK, Jo, we have water — on!' yelled Ray, barely audible over the deafening crackle of flames. As the fire consumed the burning aviation fuel it was gaining strength, causing countless pops, whizzes and bangs as it destroyed everything in its path. Trying to keep a cool head, I opened and closed the branch by twisting it on and off. This was a test to ensure strong water pressure was coming through, and also to make sure it worked once I got really close to the fire. If it didn't, I stood no chance of outrunning it. Thank God, I thought, as I felt the water surge through the charged hose, bringing it to life.

I crouched low and gritted my teeth as I turned the branch to 'on' and moved steadily closer. This was it; there were no safety nets here. The wind had picked up speed, and was now blowing so hard I could barely see. My eyes started to sting as the wind caught my own water spray and blew it straight back at me in a filthy, baking hot vapour cloud. I tried not to breathe it in, keeping my head down as a slippery oil slick of petroleum and water formed under my feet.

Desperately, I held on to the hose. I knew I couldn't drop or damage it, and used all my strength to hold it firmly, crooking it under my right arm with my left arm braced over the top to make an arm lock. With Ray directly behind me and the others ensuring the water flow was constant, we were working together in perfect harmony.

I knew I could hold this position for some time, and as I built up confidence, I inched forwards, spraying water continuously in an arcing motion from left to right. I will get this fire under control, I said to myself. I will put it out. As I did so, I was filled with an all-consuming adrenalin rush. I felt as though I'd tapped into some internal superpower that boosted my heart rate, gave me greater strength and dramatically heightened my senses. Who knew fighting fires could be such fun? To keep myself calm, I focused my mind inwards. The Eurythmics were in the charts with 'Sweet Dreams (Are Made of This)' and as the blaze roared in front of me, I started singing it to myself. Oh, if Annie Lennox could see me now, I thought to myself.

In twenty brutal, brilliant minutes, the blaze was out. As the last flames subsided and the heat died down I held my position, making certain that there was nothing left burning before edging closer to the glowing tanker. As the last flickers died out, Barry called a halt to the exercise by waving his arms and calling out to us loudly, 'OK, your work is done. Well done, that wasn't an easy task. I have to say you've all done really well. I will be contacting Bruce Hogg, your Chief Fire Officer, to let him know how you did.'

As he dismissed us, Ray gave me a friendly nudge. 'Wow! That was bloody great, wasn't it?' I was ecstatic, and smiled over to him and the rest of our happy crew. We must have done well, I reckoned, as I saw even Matthew give me a quiet thumbs up. I felt like Queen of the Universe! It was only when I looked down at myself — filthy, wet, muddy and stinking of burning oil — I realized that maybe I didn't look like it. 'You look a right state,' said Ray, laughing. But I couldn't have cared less. All I needed was ten minutes to recover along with my faithful props — a bottle of Lucozade and a roll-up — and I'd be right as rain. As my head hit the pillow that night my mind was still racing. 'Sweet Dreams' was still going round in a loop in my head. But so was the visceral thrill of facing down a fire. You can keep your nine to five, two point five kids and house in the suburbs, I thought.

Sweet dreams were made of *this*.

7

Every Breath You Take

Dense, suffocating smoke filled my nose, ears, eyes and mouth. I couldn't see, smell, speak or breathe. As the toxic fumes filled my lungs and I gasped desperately for air, I could feel my life force slowly ebbing away. So this was it. I was dying. And in, of all places, the turbine room of a greasy, dirty power station in the arse-end of Great Yarmouth. As I slowly slipped from consciousness, I could dimly hear Graeme's voice calling my name. Graeme? What was he doing here? Wait a minute . . . 'Jo, Jo . . . wake up! You're going to be late.'

★   ★   ★

It was the second week of our long awaited (read: 'dreaded') breathing apparatus (BA) course, and it's fair to say the pressure was getting to me. No longer did I fall into a deep, uninterrupted sleep the second I turned the light out, waking up feeling bright-eyed and bushy-tailed. Now my nights were erratic, sweat-drenched affairs filled with nightmarish visions of stifling, smoke-filled rooms and a terrifying fear of suffocation.

It had all started innocently enough, ten days earlier.

'OK, listen up, you lot. I've got some news for you,' said Paul Holmes breezily as we sat dozing in the classroom one afternoon at Wymondham. 'The next three weeks will be spent on the breathing apparatus course. This won't be easy. You will be pushed harder than you've ever been pushed before, and if you fail it, there's no ifs or buts — you'll fail the entire course. Which will mean the last thirteen months will have all been for nothing.' If I wasn't paying attention before, I was listening now. 'I guarantee that these will be the toughest weeks of your lives. You'll also be with a new set of instructors, so we won't be there to hold your hand if things get difficult — which they will.' At this point I heard myself take an audible gulp. 'If you've got any sense, I advise you to be in peak physical shape. Because you're going to need your wits about you.' I'd already heard stories about how tough the BA course was, and vowed I wouldn't screw up at this late stage. After so long cooped up at Wymondham, I was desperate to start work at a real-life fire station. If I had to pass one final test to get there then fine — bring it on.

The course was led by a grey-haired instructor called George Harvey. This was bad news. An ex-Navy man, Harvey took us for marching practice. Spit would spray everywhere as we stomped up and down the drill yard while he yelled abuse at us. The thought of three entire weeks spent under his iron rule made my heart sink.

However, as Officer in Charge of Breathing Apparatus for the entire Norfolk Fire Service, Harvey understood that this role demanded a different approach to his usual drill-them-until-they-drop approach.

'Good morning, junior firefighters,' he said in measured tones I'd never heard him use before. 'I am here to teach you everything you need to know about how you use compressed air breathing apparatus. Before you get your hands on any of the equipment, however, you will be shown some instructional films explaining how procedures have evolved and improved over the years. Please pay attention — what you learn from them might just save your life.'

As the blinds were closed and the overhead projector whirred into life, I felt myself being transported through time as a series of short films highlighted the hard lessons learned from the brigade's worst disasters. The most notorious was at London's Smithfield Meat Market in January 1958, a colossal fire that blazed for three days and spread through 2.5 acres of underground passages. It took 1,700 firefighters and 389 appliances to get it under control. Tragically, two officers — Jack Fort-Wells and Dick Stocking — had died when they had run out of air while fighting the fire in the labyrinthine basement. 'It was a maze,' recalled John Bishop, one of the first firefighters on the scene. 'All we could find were passageways with meat packed either side from floor to ceiling. The smoke got thicker — you could eat it; black oily smoke. It was very cold down there and you were cold, even though you were sweating. That was fear.' It was appalling to think of these two brave 'smoke-eaters' dying in such circumstances, and after the outcry that followed, the London Fire Brigade took steps to improve BA procedure to ensure a greater margin of safety.

The next incident was even more affecting, but for very different reasons. This one involved a fire at RAF Neatishead in Norfolk, a radar centre established during the Second World War. In February 1966 a fire broke out in the main bunker in which three firefighters lost their lives, including Divisional Officer James William Todd who was awarded the

British Empire Medal for gallantry. As soon as this name came up on screen, I felt a shiver run through me. This was the medal I'd seen in the glass cabinet at Whitegates before my first interview. It was humbling to think I was following in his footsteps.

Having been successfully catapulted out of our comfort zone, Harvey explained the various procedures necessary when using breathing apparatus. On any job, various lines (ropes) would be used. To begin with, a main BA guideline 100 metres long would be used, off which additional branch-lines would be connected.

To ensure everyone's safety in such hazardous conditions, a control (or 'tally') board would also need to be manned by a designated BA Entry Control Officer wearing an armband. These 'tallies' were plastic discs that each firefighter would be given. Their own individual tally would then be carefully copied onto the board with their personal details and their time of entry. Far from being the easy option, this was an incredibly stressful job that involved monitoring the movements of up to twelve firefighters at a time, while calculating how long their air would last.

The longer the week went on, the more I realized that using the BA was like a job in itself. As well as learning new procedures and mind-boggling facts about the effect of heat on the body's ability to sweat and cool down, came a whole set of new equipment.

'Right, Jo, it's about time we got you dressed and ready for action,' said Harvey, gesturing to the pile of cylinders, compressors and other unrecognizable tools on the table in front of him. I was conscious that the weight of the 17-kilogram steel cylinder might be too much for me, and was relieved when he gave me a hand. 'This is the one and only time I will help you put the set on,' he added, as if reading my thoughts. 'After that, you're on your own.'

As I squirmed under the grip of the chest-straps, I thanked God for being the most flat-chested girl I knew. I then fastened the waistband tightly so that the entire weight of the steel cylinder was securely attached to my back. Miraculously, it wasn't as heavy as I thought it would be. I then pulled on the neoprene face mask, attaching the mouth-piece and pulling the straps over my head to create a complete seal around my head. After I'd practised how to draw any air into the unit by sucking hard on the mouthpiece to create a vacuum, my visor was blacked out using a shower cap. I couldn't see a thing. I couldn't hear anything either, other than the rasping sound of my own breath reverberating inside the mask.

Completely disoriented, I started to do what Harvey had dubbed the 'Mickey Mouse' shuffle across the room. This consisted of me putting my weight on my weaker left foot, then sweeping across and outwards with my right foot, making an arc in front of me as I felt for obstacles. As I was doing this, I kept my right hand pinned flat with the palm facing outwards, against the wall. This was to prevent any instinctive grasping at anything in my path — as George Harvey reminded me, if it were a live electrical cable, this would result in instant electrocution. My left hand, meanwhile, was moving up and down in front of my visor in a slow, wide sweeping motion.

After twenty minutes of fumbling, stumbling and general clumsiness, Harvey had seen enough. 'Not bad for a first attempt,' he said, as I returned to my seat and — with a growing sense of relief — watched each of the boys being equally clumsy as they were put through their paces.

'If that's what it's like in a room we've been sat in for thirteen months, what's it going to be like somewhere we've never been before?' asked Ray as he sat back down.

'Bloody impossible, I'd say,' I replied, gloomily.

The next day, Harvey led us out to the large wooden shed in one corner of the drill yard. A cavernous barn-like structure used to store equipment, it was home to the assorted junk we'd use in our daily drills. It was impossible to navigate even in broad daylight, so I shuddered to think what a balls-up we would make of it in pitch darkness. 'OK, folks, party time. In you go, one by one,' said Harvey, as clouds of smoke were pumped into it from large green canisters. 'We have a 'persons reported' inside the building. They've been in there ten minutes already, so get your skates on. We don't want that casualty dead because you're too bloody slow!'

Thick black fumes assaulted my senses as I found myself immersed in a hot, grimy, coal-black interior. Carefully following the guideline and diligently doing the 'Mickey Mouse' shuffle, I scoured the shed until I stumbled upon the 75-kilogram canvas sand dummy propped up in one corner. Using all of my strength, I hauled it out of the shed, retracing my steps using the guideline. 'Friggin' hell, Ray,' I said, eyes streaming, lungs burning, and sweating like I'd just run a mile through the Sahara in a boiler suit. 'That was meant to be one of the easy drills. Can you imagine what they're going to be like when they get harder?'

I could always rely on Ray to back me up or reassure me when the occasion demanded. 'You do know that these guys are crazy, don't you?' he said with a grin. 'Just let them have their fun, and whatever you do, don't give up.'

A week later we were driven to the Norfolk and Norwich Hospital on St Stephen's Street. I passed this magnificent red brick building, dating back to the 1770s, each day on my way to work and had never given it a second thought. As we descended into its vast basement, I realized this was — like Smithfields — exactly the kind of labyrinth where things could go horribly wrong.

A century's worth of rusty bed frames, medical cabinets and, most unnervingly, model human skeletons appeared to have been left to rot down there, and as black smoke once more billowed from the large green canisters, I felt a ghastly sense of unease. With Matthew manning the control board at the entrance, Ray, Stuart and I attempted to lay a guideline. As we crashed into the countless bed frames, discarded chairs and cabinets, however, it became clear we were hopelessly underprepared. It was an impossible task, and felt like one that had been designed for us to fail. 'What fucking happened to you in there?' roared Harvey at no one in particular when we finally emerged, dazed, confused and with our tails firmly between our legs.

'Sorry, sir?' I replied.

'I *said*, what the fuck just happened to you down there? Shall we stop the course and send you all home? Because you don't seem to have grasped anything that you've been taught. Maybe I should go over to that old people's home across the road and see if they can do any better! For fuck's sake. Wake up. Improve or . . . ' He shook his head as he walked away. He didn't have to tell us what the alternative was. It was 'shape up or ship out' time. If this was designed as shock therapy, it worked. Over the next three weeks the tests continued, but each came with a clear structure and a sense that if we kept our heads, we could complete the task.

We rescued 'victims' from huge grain silos at King's Lynn and the power station at Great Yarmouth, cut our way through razor-sharp barbed wire at the old Nissen huts at Croxton and waded through sewers 18 metres below Norwich city centre in chemical protection suits surrounded by rats the size of cats. As I got more comfortable with the equipment, I began to love using it. Putting the mask on felt like being cocooned in your own bubble, and working against the clock to solve a puzzle added an element of danger I thrived on. Although even I was worried about our final assessment, which we were told would focus on 'heat and humidity'.

I had seen some large red 'pods' similar to oil tanks at the brigade headquarters at Hethersett, and never been sure of their exact purpose. So when I saw that they had been positioned ominously on the drill yard, it could only mean one thing.

'Right, recruits, this is your final test,' explained Harvey, a knowing grin plastered on his face. 'The pod in front of you will shortly be filled with steam. Your job is to locate the foam canisters inside and use them to build the blue and black chequered pattern at the far end until it is complete. All the time you are in there, you will be asked questions to monitor your mental agility as you complete the task.'

It sounded like some sadistic spin-off from *It's a Knockout*. However, as I was weighed and ushered towards the entrance wearing a full chemical protection suit including gloves, I realized this was the most serious test of all. I knew that the canisters weighed 25 kilograms each when full, and lifting them into place in stifling heat wasn't going to be easy.

As I entered I was immediately hit by an overwhelming wall of heat. This wasn't like walking into an oven, I thought to myself. I was *actually* walking into an oven. As I began moving the canisters into place, the questions started up, bellowed by George Harvey as he stood at the entrance.

'What's your date of birth?'

'Twenty-eighth of March 1965, sir!'

'Who is your Chief Fire Officer?'

'Chief Fire Officer Hogg, sir!'

'What is your mother's maiden name?'

'Carter, sir!'

We'd already learned that excessive exposure to steam makes the body stop sweating and overheat, and as the minutes ticked by, I felt on the verge of passing out. This wasn't a test, I said bitterly to myself, this was torture. After thirty-five agonizing minutes, it was over. My brain felt like a nuclear power plant had exploded inside of it, my lungs, arms and legs like I'd run back-to-back marathons. I saw a vision of a million castaways begging for water — they weren't half as thirsty as I was.

'Good work, Reynolds,' said Harvey, after I'd composed myself, been weighed again and handed a saline solution to counteract the loss in body weight. He didn't need to say anything else. I'd passed.

Back at The Laurels, news of my triumph over seemingly insurmountable odds was greeted with blank expressions.

'That shit sounds heavy,' said Adrian vaguely, when I told him what I'd been through over the last three weeks. 'Walking into a container full of steam, that must have been trippy.' I wasn't expecting a surprise party in my honour, but I was still a bit put out. As I surveyed the piles of washing-up festering in the sink, my high spirits drained away. I was slowly realizing that I was growing apart from my housemates. Mick had started going missing for weeks on end, only to return from solitary benders looking like he'd been to hell and back, while Adrian seemed to spend his life in a dope-fuelled daze. My relationship with Graeme was suffering, too.

Despite still indulging in the occasional binge together, I knew I wasn't the same carefree soul who had toured the pubs with him on my arrival in Norwich. Work was becoming my priority.

As I walked into the sitting room, which, as usual, was a minefield of leftover dinner plates and empty beer cans, I heard a sickening crunch. I had accidentally stepped on a dozing Claude, who had passed out from the fumes from another marathon smoking session. It was the final straw. The next evening, I told the others I would be moving out when our tenancy agreement ran out. 'OK,' said Mick, as he toked on a spliff, eyes still glued to his favourite show, *Crossroads*. 'Put the kettle on, Jo, would you?'

It was time to grow up.

8

Prince Charming

After fifteen strength-sapping months, the day I'd been waiting for had finally arrived. I'd made it to the moment all recruits live for: Passing Out Parade. To mark the occasion, a smart little blue programme of events had even been printed. I picked it up from the kitchen table and ran my finger over the colour image of the Norfolk Fire Service crest on the cover. I'd come a long way from the wide-eyed ingénue who had first been captivated by that same eight-sided badge in the glass cabinet at Whitegates. But did I really possess those eight qualities any firefighter must have: tact, perseverance, gallantry, loyalty, dexterity, explicitness, observation and sympathy? My reverie was broken by the sound of the phone ringing in the hall. I knew the others would ignore it, so, even though I was already halfway out the door, I thought I'd better answer.

'Hello, Firefighter Reynolds here,' I said jokingly into the receiver, presuming that whoever was on the other end of the line would soon be joining me at Wymondham.

'Hello . . . is that Josephine Reynolds?' asked a reedy voice at the other end of the line. I felt my hackles rise.

No one had called me Josephine since my mum when she used to give me a ticking-off at Ben-y-Mar.

'Who's calling, please?'

'That's really not important. I'm just wondering if you could confirm that today is your Passing Out Parade at Wymondham.'

'Well, as a matter of fact it is,' I said, 'But . . . '

Before I could say any more, the line went dead. Strange, I thought. Perhaps I had a mystery admirer? I put it out of my mind, closed the door behind me and ran over to my trusty Avenger parked outside — best not be late, today of all days.

* * *

By the time we had assembled on the drill yard, immaculate in full firefighting uniform, the early morning mist had cleared, revealing a crisp autumn day. As I stood to attention — chin up, chest out, shoulders back, stomach in — I could see my mum, dad and Malcy waving from the makeshift grandstand that had been constructed for friends and

106

family. I forced myself not to wave back. Sitting alongside them were the entire Norfolk Fire Service top brass: Chief Fire Officer Hogg, Anthony Hood, Chairman of the Norfolk Fire Committee, Raymond Frostick, Chairman of Norfolk County Council, plus all of our other instructors, all in full regimental clobber.

To mark the occasion, our dreary drill yard had been transformed into, if not quite a Hollywood sound stage, then a passable recreation of the average high street. We had been practising specific drills for weeks, each set in mocked-up buildings with painted signs called 'The Grand Hotel', 'Fish & Chip Shop' and 'Fred's Garage'.

The formal programme of events read as follows: 1445: Demonstration by Recruits
1) Hose and Hydrant Drill
2) Drill (simulating small fire in a shop)
3) Breathing Apparatus and High Expansion Foam Drill (simulating garage fire)
4) Finale, Large Hotel Fire

All of which must have sounded quite impressive. However, such was our focus and determination not to mess up, we did each one almost without thinking, the two hours of drills passing in a blur of running, hose, ladders, smoke and BA work. No longer was I shy, weak and unsure of myself. After fifteen months of intense training, I felt fit, confident and, most importantly, that I'd earned the right to be there.

It was only afterwards, when we were called forward to greet the assembled VIPs, that the nerves kicked in. As I walked across the yard towards the line of dignitaries, I prayed I wouldn't trip up and collapse in a heap at their feet. 'Congratulations, Firefighter Reynolds. Very well done indeed,' said Anthony Hood, handing me certificates confirming my proficiency in first aid, lifesaving and the use of breathing apparatus. 'Quite a supreme effort, you should be proud of your hard work.' As he said this, he leaned over, and, bending beneath my yellow cork helmet, planted a kiss on my cheek. I struggled to keep my composure. Did he really just do that? This wasn't the fire service I was used to!

There was one final ritual to complete. Throughout training, we had worn red sleeves on our shoulder epaulettes to denote we were junior firefighters. Now these could be removed once and for all. As the five of us threw them into the air in celebration, I watched mine arc in slow motion against the dazzling blue sky. You've done it, I said silently to myself. You're a firefighter now.

'Do you want to know a secret?' said Eddie to me afterwards, sidling up as I mingled with the guests sipping tea and munching on triangular sandwiches. 'I always knew you'd make it. There were a few wobbles along the way, granted, but you'll make a bloody good firefighter. You'll get a pay rise too, so I'm hoping it means we'll see the back of that clapped-out Avenger.'

I was ecstatic. No longer was I at a Passing Out Parade for junior firefighters in what was, essentially, a car park in a remote corner of Norfolk. In my mind's eye, I was Belle of the Ball, waving to thousands of well-wishers from the top of a float, beaming with joy. At that precise moment, a flashbulb exploded in my face, bringing me back down to earth. 'Thanks, Jo . . . I'm from the *Eastern Daily Press*,' said a voice I instantly recognized as the same one that had rung The Laurels that morning. 'Your picture will be in the paper tomorrow.' My life was already strange. But it was about to get a whole lot stranger.

*   *   *

In the week following my Passing Out Parade, the phone never stopped ringing. Overnight, it seemed, I had gone from a lowly trainee firefighter to international superstar.

Well, not quite. But it was impossible not to feel a swelling pride as, following my appearance in the *Eastern Daily Press* (under the headline 'A Kiss for Firefighter Jo') a stream of reporters got in touch asking to write profiles on 'Britain's first female firefighter'. Having made sure that any fees I received would be sent directly to the Fire Service Benevolent Fund, I decided to embrace my newfound role as media personality. After an interview on Radio Norfolk I was photographed 'rescuing' Eddie from the Training Tower for the *Daily Telegraph*, appeared on the BBC's six o'clock news and was even interviewed on the village green outside The Laurels by the nice man from the *Daily Express* (I thought it was probably best not to invite him in for a cup of tea).

Despite all this exposure, I still wasn't prepared for the phone call from someone claiming to be from TV-am. This was the country's biggest breakfast television show, watched by 3 million viewers — including my dad and Jean. The researcher explained that they'd seen me on the BBC news and that 'Chris' was very keen to meet me. By Chris, I knew she was referring to Chris Tarrant, the show's host, and a hero of mine ever since

Malcy and I had laughed ourselves senseless watching him throw custard pies in people's faces on the Saturday morning children's show *Tiswas*. 'So, Jo, what I'm asking is, would you like to appear on TV-am tomorrow?'

Did I want to? Of course I did! For all my training, I was still a naïve country girl whose only knowledge of the capital was gawping out of the window at Big Ben as the coach to Norwich left Victoria. So when I turned up at the studios of TV-am in Camden the next day — my train fare and transport all pre-arranged — I was more nervous than I'd ever been in my life. My jitters weren't helped when I clapped eyes on my fellow guest.

'Erm . . . excuse me, but isn't that Adam Ant?' I said to the assistant who had ushered me through the rabbit warren of offices and into a brightly lit TV studio.

'Yes . . . he's going to be on the show with you,' she said breezily, as I felt my knees wobbling beneath me.

Oh . . . my . . . God. If I was nervous already, this was a whole new dimension of panic. I had idolized Adam ever since I'd first clapped eyes on his warpaint-covered features performing 'Ant Music' on *Top of the Pops*. The sight of him in the flesh was almost too much. To make matters worse, he was decked out in his complete 'Prince Charming' regalia of frock coat, spangly trousers and thigh-high boots. I, on the other hand, was wearing my full firefighter's uniform as requested, complete with thick black coat and bright yellow helmet. All in all, not my sexiest outfit. We looked like we'd both come straight from a fancy dress party, but no one batted an eyelid as we were directed towards the show's famous salmon-pink sofa.

'Are you feeling comfortable, Jo?' asked a harassed-looking woman in a headset as the countdown to show time started and the studio light flickered from green to red. 'Well, actually . . . ' Before I could finish, she had darted off, talking frantically into her headset microphone. Seconds before the show started, Chris Tarrant appeared. I suddenly felt very nervous. What did he have planned for the interview? I already felt like an idiot in my firefighter's uniform, and he obviously wasn't going to make fun of my co-star.

Having politely interrogated Adam about his latest single, Chris turned his attention towards me, explaining to the viewers that he was now in the presence of Britain's first female firefighter. 'So, Jo, you're eighteen years old. What on earth made you want you to join the fire service?' As he said the words, the cameras swivelled in my direction, and I could feel every one of the 3 million viewers at home looking up from their cornflakes in curiosity. Who was this girl? For a second, my mind went blank. Should I say something flippant? *Well, Chris, the truth is . . . I only did it so I could hang around with lots of dishy firemen all day.* Or maybe I should be serious? *Well, Chris, I've always been a staunch feminist . . .* Instead, I heard myself explaining that the fire service had been the only job available to an inexperienced seventeen-year-old country girl who had barely scraped four O-levels.

Judging by the glazed look on Chris's face, this wasn't what he wanted to hear. Even the cameramen looked bored. 'I think what most people are wondering is whether you're actually strong enough to do what is, essentially, a man's job,' he said, a devilish grin forming on his lips. Where was this leading? Time to up the stakes.

'Well, I could put you over my shoulder, no problem,' I shot back. 'Do you want me to prove it?' Before Chris could get a word out, I stood up from the couch, dropped my shoulder and pulled his body towards me in a fireman's lift. Chris's groin was now closer to my face than it really ought to have been on live television, and within seconds he was over my shoulder as I stood up to my full height. It was a maneouvre I'd done every day for the last fifteen months, and judging by his stunned silence, he'd been winded in the process — yes, the infamous Chris Tarrant talking machine had finally been silenced!

The next question was, what to do with him? To be honest I didn't have a clue. But as Adam smiled and the cameras followed me, I strode purposefully towards the studio exit. *A woman can do this job*, I wanted to yell down the camera when I finally put him down to cheers from the audience. *I've just proved it.* Thankfully, Chris took his unexpected upending in the right spirit. Afterwards, after a few congratulations from the backroom staff, I left the studio — still wearing my firefighter's uniform.

'That was classic!' said Graeme when I rang him from a pay phone at the station on the way back to Norwich, desperate for reassurance. 'I've never seen Chris Tarrant be lost for words before.' I felt I'd made a point, and hopefully made a few people smile. But little did I know that, in the wider world, my little display had made some people as mad as hell.

★ ★ ★

The letter arrived the following week. On the surface, it looked innocuous enough. Addressed to 'Miss Jo Reynolds, The Laurels, Village Green, Pulham Market, England', with a blue 'Air Mail' sticker and a postmark reading 'White Rock, British Columbia', it even looked faintly exotic compared to the final demands that usually landed on the doormat.

Perhaps, I thought, a rich aunt in Canada has died, leaving me all her worldly possessions? As I tore the seal, I could already see the newspaper headlines: 'Firefighter Jo Quits Force Following Shock 'Maple Leaf Millions' Windfall'.

'It's like a dream,' I'd tell reporters. 'One minute you're crawling through sewers on eleven pounds a week, the next you're living on a yacht in St Tropez.'

Instead, what I found inside made my blood run cold. On a small square of white paper, someone had written the words 'Good Luck in Your New Job' in black ink, and attached it to a newspaper cutting with the heading 'People'. This is how it read:

Los Angeles firemen made a female paramedic trainee shave her pubic hair in a hazing ritual, and now she's $75,000 richer. Sally Byrne, one of three female

115

trainees in 1978, sued the city and won. She said firemen told her it was a common initiation rite for trainees to shave their pubic hair and if she didn't do it, they would. Eventually she gave in. When word got out, five firemen and a captain were suspended. Then Byrne quit because they blamed her for the suspensions.

At first, I dismissed it as a sick joke. If people wanted to get their kicks trying to intimidate me, let them go ahead and try. But as the days went by I saw it more as a reflection of an ingrained attitude towards women's role in society. I had been intrigued by the media coverage a few months earlier of the so-called Greenham Common Women. These were 70,000 ordinary women who had formed a 14-mile human chain around an RAF base in Berkshire in protest at the decision to base 96 Tomahawk Cruise missiles there — each one, four times more powerful than the bomb that obliterated Hiroshima. Rather than demonstrate in the traditional way, they had hung brightly coloured scarves, ribbons, photos and family mementoes (baby clothes; kids' toys) on the fences to highlight the possible loss of innocent life. This seemed entirely reasonable to me, and the hostile press they received made my blood boil. According to the tabloids, these 'ban-the-bomb mums' should have been at home fixing the tea rather than worrying about the future of the planet. So much for female emancipation! It seemed that it was OK for us to have a woman prime minister because she was part of a much larger 'boys' club' and obeyed their rules. But if any regular woman challenged her pre-conceived role, she could expect to be taken down a peg or two.

I'd never considered myself a feminist, but I couldn't help but see myself as another woman who was out on a limb. Even before all the press attention, I'd been very conscious that women firefighters were as rare as hen's teeth. Ever since I'd joined up, Chief Officer Hogg had sent me articles about the (admittedly slow) progress being made to employ women in brigades outside Norfolk. One article from the West Midlands Fire Service magazine *Firepower* revealed that, of the 1,200 applications to join their brigade in 1983, only four came from women. Three of those sat the written exam, but neither of the two who passed turned up for the two-day physical test. Consequently, there were still no female firefighters serving in the West Midlands or Warwickshire (or, as far as I was aware, anywhere else). Was this because they didn't feel they could do the work, or because they didn't feel welcome?

One article in particular from the *Liverpool Daily Post* made me feel uneasy. Headlined 'Rights That Are Not Fire Proof', it featured a large picture of yours truly carrying a hose reel, with the headline: 'In the hot seat: what harassment does the job hold for workers like Britain's first firewoman, Josephine Reynolds?' They'd cribbed the picture from the *Daily Telegraph* article, but the content was very different.

The article explained that a historic lawsuit had just been brought by New York's first two women firefighters against the city's all-male fire department following their dismissal. In a scathing ruling, the (female) judge had ordered the reinstatement of the two women, Brenda Berkman and Zaida Gonzalez, citing 'extraordinary' evidence of intentional discrimination and 'distressing proof' of sexual harassment. The details were shocking. Berkman stated in court that 'I've had death threats and so many 3 a.m. phone calls that I had to get an unlisted number,' explaining that her male co-workers refused to eat with, swap shifts or even talk to her, even about what kind of fires she was going to. Ms Gonzalez appeared to have had it even worse. Judge Sifton noted: 'Prophylactic devices and a wet vibrator were left in her bed, her earrings, underwear and badge were stolen from her locker, her helmet disappeared and once she discovered her air hose had been disconnected from her air tank.' And all this despite the fact both Berkman and Gonzalez had passed all the standardized tests set for them — just as I had. Most depressing were the comments by a union official called Tom Gates about their height — both were 5 feet 7 inches tall. 'These little women are what my father calls 'circus freaks',' he said. 'I call them defective equipment. They are as dangerous on the job as a frayed rope. It is the men who have to pick up the slack.' Was this the kind of intimidation I was about to face?

I knew that starting work as a fully fledged firefighter was a big step up from being a trainee. I'd already started to see my time at Wymondham as a big adventure, the kind of experience that would have us clutching our sides at reunions in twenty years' time (*'Hey guys, remember what fun it was carrying the Coventry Climax to the river and back in 100-degree heat? And what about Gallagher? What a guy!'*). Would my new workmates understand me in the way my instructors had? Or would I be in for the kind of rough ride Berkman and Gonzalez had experienced?

I knew I could pull my weight and take responsibility for other people's lives, but would I be treated as an equal? As a firefighter first and a woman second?

I'd had a taste of what might lie in store for me during training. 'Please don't take this personally,' one middle-aged fireman had told me sheepishly as I sat in the mess room at Norwich station one afternoon after an exercise clearing storm drains. 'But my wife has told me that I shouldn't speak to you.' I was shocked. Was my presence really giving the womenfolk of the Norfolk Fire Service palpitations, worried that I was about to ride into town and steal their men? Either way, I couldn't help but think there was a huge collective sigh across the whole of East Anglia when word came through that I'd been offered a full-time position at Thetford Fire Station.

What was waiting for me?

I'd find out soon enough.

9

Strange Little Girl

'Well, I guess that's it then,' said Graeme. We were standing outside The Laurels on a bright but cold morning in March 1984, and it felt like more than the seasons changing. 'You're off to start your exciting new life with your firefighting buddies while we're left here plodding along in the slow lane. I'll probably never see you again. Unless it's on TV, of course.'

I looked at him shivering in his baggy green army surplus trousers and Blondie t-shirt and felt myself start to well up. 'Of course I'll see you again, you daft sod,' I said. 'I'm going to Thetford, not Mars.' I've always hated goodbyes, and I took his silence as my cue to make a hasty exit. 'Look,' I said, planting a quick kiss on his cheek before running over to my car and putting the key in the ignition, 'if you really want to get hold of me, you can always dial 999.'

As I waved goodbye, I remembered the old Graeme — the one I'd spent those glorious evenings with, driving back from gigs in his

Zephyr playing The Ramones at full blast. Underneath the shaggy haircut and five o'clock shadow, he was still pretty much the same scruffy but loveable guy who had taken me under his wing when I'd shown up on Dad and Jean's doorstep. It was me who had changed. I was no longer an innocent, wet-behind-the-ears-sixteen-year-old. I was a trained firefighter, with, potentially, a long career in the fire service ahead of me. For all the laughs we'd had at The Laurels, I was glad to be leaving. I was tired of waking up in my freezing cold bedroom with its mismatched curtains and creaking floorboards and coming home to find the coffee jar decimated, no loo roll and the washing-up still not done.

It was time to start a new chapter in my new life.

I'd been to see the bank manager and put a deposit down on a sweet little flint cottage on Ford Street, just around the corner from where I'd be working. At £13,000, it seemed crazily expensive — my mortgage payments would last forever — but I'd fallen in love with it on sight. A classic two-up two-down close to the river with a white front door and sash windows, it also had a small outdoor area where I could keep my new pushbike, which I planned to use for my short commute to and from work.

★ ★ ★

I had furnished the house with assorted castoffs from friends and family, and the result looked like a schizophrenic cross between a yuppie bachelorette pad and a student house. Fat, over-stuffed sofa from the 1930s? Tick! Hideous floral fire-screen? Tick! Glass-top coffee table with stubby chrome legs? Tick! But it was all mine, and best of all, any correspondence from headquarters came grandly addressed to: Firewoman J. D. Reynolds, 3 Ford Street, Thetford, Norfolk. My transition from scatty teenager to independent young woman was finally complete.

After all the nerve-jangling anticipation, my first week at work was reassuringly low-key. Far from encountering a bunch of sexist pigs ruthlessly plotting my downfall, my new colleagues were down-to-earth family men who hid their curiosity behind a veil of polite good manners. This sense of calm and common decency stemmed from the top down. A ruggedly good-looking six-footer with twinkling eyes, shoulder-length black hair and the voice of a late-night radio DJ, my new boss was aptly called Nigel Monument.

As Sub Officer (usually abbreviated to 'Sub-O' or just 'Sub') Nigel was responsible for the day-today running of Thetford. His easygoing manner, however, belied a natural authority.

When he spoke, everyone listened, a waft of smoke from his licorice roll-up our cue to leap into action. Each morning as he arrived, firing off a volley of brisk good mornings in his rich Norfolk burr, the mood of the station shifted imperceptibly — you could almost hear the cogs beginning to whir. Nigel did things his own way. Morning roll call was held, not standing to attention in the yard, but over a cup of tea in the lecture room. Our daily tasks — checking the oil, wheels and lights of the station's two pumps, scrubbing the forecourt, sweeping the yard — were allotted calmly, with a minimum of fuss. I would soon learn all about his deadpan sense of humour, but for now, I was just pleased to have a boss who would give me a fair crack of the whip.

'Let's get things straight from the start, Jo,' he said on my first day, pouring two steaming mugs of tea in his office. 'The way I see it, you've clearly satisfied all your instructors at training school and know how to work the equipment. You've come out the other end and been assigned to us. It's obviously big news you coming here, and we've had the top brass round, who made sure we installed a ladies' toilet and ensured all our facilities were up to scratch. Now it's our job to work with you. We've got a good bunch of lads here, so I can't envisage any problems.'

As a day-manning station, Thetford always had six or seven full-time firefighters on duty. It was unoccupied at night, however, which sadly meant that there was no fireman's pole. Instead, it operated on an 'alerter' system (known to everyone simply as 'bleepers'). This was a matchbox-sized device each firefighter was provided with. If a 'shout' came through from HQ, it would go off at any time of the day or night, 24/7,365 days a year. It was then a question of getting to the station quickly enough to make it onto the pump. Five minutes was the rule — get there any later and you were failing in your duties.

'There's around twenty retained firemen who live locally,' Nigel explained. 'They only get paid for the jobs they attend, so they're usually pretty quick off the mark if their bleeper goes off. So if I were you, I'd get your skates on if you want to see some action.' After a few more preliminaries, his face broke out into a crinkly smile.

'OK, I think we've covered all bases. Now,

to the really important stuff . . . one lump, or two?'

★ ★ ★

My new workmates were a mixed bag of old timers (or 'senior hands'), edging their way towards retirement, and younger guys working their way up the career ladder. I knew it would take me a good while to penetrate this cliquey boys' club, so in the meantime I soaked up the surroundings, desperate for clues on how to behave.

It was a minefield. Everything, it seemed, involved some kind of hierarchy. In the mess room — where a television was permanently tuned to the snooker — each crew member had their own favourite chair. Sitting in someone's else's seat appeared tantamount to murdering their offspring, and I quickly learned to ask if it was OK before I took the weight off my feet. The canteen also seemed to have its own set of rules. This was run by a twinkly-eyed Irish lady in her forties called Mary. At one o'clock each day, after much banging and crashing of pots and pans, the hatch would open, cutlery would be scattered on the Formica tables and there would be a hearty cry of 'Come and get it!' at which point everyone would abandon what they were doing and line up at the hatch to be fed.

'And what delights have we in store today, Mary?' asked a burly man in front of me on my second day as a mouth-watering aroma drifted from the kitchen. 'Cottage pie, with all the trimmings,' she said, piling a mountain of food onto his plate. 'That little lot will be followed by sponge pudding and custard. I hope that's satisfactory?' I stared agog at the amount of food on his plate. Was rationing about to be introduced? As I nervously approached the hatch, thankfully Mary gave me a broad smile. 'A-ha! Firefighter Reynolds, I presume,' she said. 'I saw you on the television a few months ago. You gave me and my other half a right laugh. I think you and me are going to get along just fine.'

I smiled meekly as she ladled scalding hot gravy onto my already overflowing plate, but I was secretly delighted. Mary was a formidable figure, and would be a strong ally when the testosterone started flying around.

★   ★   ★

As we did our daily familiarization manoeuvres around the town, visiting local businesses and checking water hydrants, I learned a little more about Thetford itself.

A pretty market town dating back to the

Domesday Book, it was surrounded by the biggest man-made forest in Britain. This artfully constructed patchwork of slender pines and flat heathland looked, I thought, like something out of Grimm's Fairy Tales, and I made the stupid mistake of saying so one afternoon in the mess room.

'Grim — that's the word, all right,' growled a gnarled senior hand called Ronnie Bass from behind his copy of *Sporting Life*. 'I'll have you know those woods are the number one suicide spot in this part of Norfolk. I've seen more dead bodies in there than you've had hot dinners. Teenage mums, stressed-out businessmen, blokes with gambling debts — they all look normal enough when they drive in. But they all come out the same way . . . dead.'

He hadn't spoken a word to me before now and I must have looked slightly startled at this outburst because Ronnie put his newspaper down on the table in front of him and came over to where I was sitting. 'Look, sorry if I was a bit abrupt just then,' he said, his face softening. 'It's just you see a lot of things in this job and it toughens you up. You don't see the beauty in things so easily, if you get my drift.'

As we got talking, Ronnie explained that he'd been a fireman for the last twenty-five years, and had seen the job requirements change radically 'When I started out, it was all about chimney fires,' he said almost wistfully 'You would go out at least once a day. We'd push old split canes up people's chimneys and pump water from old wartime stirrup pumps to put the fire out. Then central heating came along and all the chimney fires, bar the odd one, disappeared. But as cars got faster and roads got wider, road accidents replaced them as the bread-and-butter job of the fireman or, I should say, firefighter.'

It was fascinating to hear about the dramatic changes that the service had been through in recent decades and I soaked it up like a sponge. I could happily listen to Ronnie, Nigel and the others talk for hours. It felt like there wasn't anything about the fire service I *wasn't* interested in. It was only when I returned home to Ford Street each evening that I felt the wind leave my sails.

By moving to Thetford, I'd cut myself adrift from my old friends. There was more chance of Elvis being found alive than Graeme and the others making the thirty-minute journey to see me, and I resolved to seek out a new social circle. But where to start? After a week of twiddling my thumbs, I took the plunge and dropped in at The

Dolphin, the pub at the end of the road. That was a good place to meet people, surely?

It seemed not. Most nights, I would sit alone drinking a bottle of Grolsch, my thumbs popping the white ceramic lid back and forth on its wire frame as the old boys at the bar gossiped about me. 'Is that a boy or a girl?' I'd hear, followed by a shifty half-glance. My cropped hair and tomboy style made me stand out like a sore thumb. 'Perhaps she's one of those lesbians from Greenham Common . . . '

After a couple of lonely beers, I'd wander home and dance around my little sitting room to The Pretenders, just to burn off some excess energy. No doubt the sight of me silhouetted behind the curtains must have baffled the locals still further as they staggered past at closing time.

* * *

A high-pitched shrieking noise pierced my sleep, assaulting my brain like the jab of a thousand hot needles. I stretched out an arm in the general direction of the alarm clock, flailing aimlessly until I heard it fall off the bedside cabinet and onto the floor. Still the synapse-shredding *ping-ping-ping* continued. *Shut up!* In desperation, I pulled my pillow over my ears to muffle the noise. No good. How about my pillow over my ears, and my quilt over my head? Better. What the hell was it? . . . *Oh shit!*

Within seconds I was out of bed, desperately trying not to get tangled up in my bedding as I turned off my bleeper and stumbled towards the light switch. Thank God I had carefully laid my clothes out the night before! Still in a daze, I put on my jeans, t-shirt and jumper and hurtled down the narrow staircase, dragging my bike from my tiny backyard with me out into the street.

It was just before dawn, and a grey mist hung in the air, casting eerie shadows on the pavement as I pedalled through Thetford's deserted streets. The cold air filled my lungs, waking me up, and I picked up speed as I got closer to the station. The sound of the pump's revving engine told me I still might get there in time. As cars pulled up from all directions, I hurtled past them, dumped my bike on the grass bank and grabbed my firefighting gear, jumping into the last vacant seat and slamming the door shut behind me. *I'd made it.* Then, with a shout of 'Move it, come on, *LET'S GO!*' the pump jerked forwards. We were off.

The main arterial route from Norfolk to London, the A11, was usually choc-a-bloc with traffic. At this time of day it was still deathly quiet, and from my perch on the back row familiar landmarks rushed past me in a blur, as we headed towards the outskirts of town.

During regular nine-to-five work hours, the seating positions on the fire engine were designated by number, each with a specific responsibility. But in an emergency like this, all bets were off, and I was squeezed between two men I recognized from the station but whose names I'd already forgotten — names have never been my strong point. I was glad neither said a word to me. The early start combined with the reverberations of the engine were making me feel queasy, and as I slid back and forth on my plastic seat I was grateful for the advice Ronnie Bass had given me about travelling to a job: 'Breathe properly and always look into the distance.'

Behind us, I could see Thetford's overall boss, Station Officer Frank Lane, following close behind in his fire brigade car. While we didn't have our siren on as we weren't allowed to use it at night, I could see his magnetic blue light flashing, casting strange reflections in the bushes and trees.

'So what have we got then, Sub?' asked one of the guys next to me.

'Looks like an RTA on the London Road

close to the Elveden War Memorial,' responded a voice from the front passenger seat I instantly recognized as Nigel's. 'Could be a nasty one, so keep your wits about you.'

The memorial was a famous local landmark, and I could make out the 30-metre column piercing the foggy early morning as we pulled up on a single carriageway bordered by dense woodland. I was keen to get stuck in, but as we dismounted I heard a shout: 'Jo, the Sub Officer wants you,' and saw Nigel beckoning me towards him.

I really wished he hadn't singled me out in front of the crew, especially on my first job, but I was in no position to argue as I walked over to where he was standing. 'I think you should see this before we get started,' he said, leading me towards the scene of the accident, which I could now see had blocked the entire road.

It was like a stage set from a horror film. A hundred different sensations shot through me as I tried to make sense of what my eyes were telling me. I'd rescued literally hundreds of casualties from created situations, covering almost every possible scenario, but nothing that looked like this. This was the real thing. Real people. Real wounds. Real blood.

A huge 2-tonne hay baler had skidded on the road, sending the long metal forks sticking out at the front directly into a car coming the other way. These lethal prongs had crashed through the front windscreen, neatly slicing the passenger's head in half. This macabre sight and the combined smell of metal, fuel and death sent a wave of nausea through me. It was horrific. 'If you're OK, you can get to work securing the area,' said Nigel, as I took a deep breath and set about my duties, pushing back the ever-growing slick of black motor-oil with my stiff yard-broom and sweeping up the fragments of burning metal, body tissue and shattered glass. As I did so, I pieced together what had happened as one of our guys talked to the man still trapped in the car. They were brothers who had been out night-fishing when, through a dense early morning fog, the tractor skidded across the road and hit them head-on. 'How's my brother? Please God tell me he's alive ... ' I heard him say, as I mentally blocked the words out and got on with my task, hosing down the road and shovelling soil from the grass verge on any remaining oil.

As each of the emergency services arrived on the scene, they were briefed by Nigel and set about their business. As the police breakdown vehicle removed the tractor, whose driver was unharmed, an ambulance whisked the injured man to hospital and the undertaker took the broken body to the morgue. 'OK, Jo, you can pack away now,' said Nigel in a tone of voice that told me we'd done all we could. Once all the hoses and equipment were back on the engine and the gear stowed by some unspoken signal, everyone lit cigarettes and gathered at the rear of the pump. This, I assumed, was some kind of informal debrief, and as I inhaled the nicotine and blew out a smoke ring, I marvelled at how methodical the clean-up operation had been.

One by one each problem — the blocked traffic, the trapped man, the leaking fuel tank, the dead body — had been assessed in order of importance and dealt with.

It was like clockwork. In less than an hour, the road had been cleared and the main route in and out of Norfolk had been reclaimed and reopened.

When we got back to the station, I looked at my watch. I couldn't believe that we'd accomplished so much before most people had even woken up. There was just time to go home and have a quick bath before my usual nine o'clock start. As I cycled back in, a feeling of sheer exhilaration overwhelmed me. There was no makeup on my face, my cheeks felt red and wind-burned, and my hair still stank of motor oil. But at that moment, I felt a surge of confidence run through me.

I was a firefighter now.

10

Road to Nowhere

A body was lying on my kitchen floor. As if that wasn't bad enough, it also happened to be my new boss, Nigel. And worse than that, it was all my fault.

★   ★   ★

Having negotiated my first call-out successfully, I'd begun to open up a little to my new colleagues about my life outside work. While I hadn't given them all the gory details about my lonely nights in The Dolphin, I had let slip that, a fortnight after moving in, I was still without a cooker. As a house-warming present, my dad had ordered me a second-hand Belling model, but it still hadn't arrived. As a result, I was living off food from the local garage. 'No wonder there's so little of you,' said Ronnie Bass with a chuckle as we sat in the mess room having our mid-morning coffee break. To pass the time, I thought I'd extol the virtues of what I called the 'Petrol Station Diet'.

'It's amazing,' I continued sarcastically. 'Not only do they stock the essentials — Old Holborn tobacco, Rizlas, Lucozade — they've got cuisine from around the world. I bet Delia Smith couldn't knock up anything to match the Chicken Curry flavour Pot Rice.' This made Ronnie laugh out loud, and as a few of the others looked up from watching the latest 'thrilling' encounter between Ray Reardon and Steve Davis on the TV, I decided to carry on. 'The options are limitless. You haven't lived until you've tried Smarties in a bowl of banana milk. It's just a shame it's all going to end when the cooker finally arrives on Saturday. But even then, I've still got to find someone to instal it.'

Just at that moment a waft of licorice cigarette invaded my nostrils. It was Nigel, who must have been earwigging on my ramblings from the next room. 'Well, we can't leave a damsel in distress, can we, boys?' he said. 'See you at the weekend, Jo. Just make sure the kettle's on.'

*　*　*

Three days later, I watched in a growing state of agitation as Nigel, Ronnie and another fireman called Robin Donnelly set about what on the face of it looked like a simple task. Because getting my 'new' cooker — a large, grimy appliance at least fifteen years old — through the narrow doorway into my tiny kitchen was practically impossible.

'This is like threading a camel through the eye of a needle!' gasped Ronnie, as, with one last heave, the three of them finally wedged it into place. I felt awful seeing them go to so much effort, and tried to remain upbeat as the four of us had a quick cup of tea before Ronnie and Robin said their farewells.

'OK, Jo, let's get this over with,' said Nigel, squeezing himself behind the cooker as he rummaged in his tool kit. 'Seeing as I'm boxed in here, can you go and make sure it's switched off at the fuse box? We don't want any accidents.'

Eager to please, I dashed out into the hall. Standing on tiptoes on the stairs, I flipped open the fuse box. I was met with a bewildering display of knobs and switches, none of which were labelled. After everything I'd already put Nigel through, the last thing I wanted to do was show off my ignorance of electrical circuitry. I was supposed to be a firefighter! Inwardly I cursed not having paid more attention in the classroom at Wymondham and, making an (un) educated guess, flicked the most likely looking switch to the 'OFF' position.

'It's OK, I've done it!' I yelled.

'OK, Jo, are you sure?'

'OK, Nigel — yes, I'm sure!'

BOO-OOOSH! A split second later, I watched in horror as Nigel flew across the kitchen. Two hundred and thirty volts of electricity had shot through his body, catapulting him into the air before depositing him in a heap on the lino-covered floor.

As I gazed down at his prone shape from my perch on the stairs, my blood turned to ice. Oh Christ, I've killed him. Just as I was visualizing myself being led away in handcuffs, I noticed a facial muscle twitch. Yes, there it was again. A couple of seconds later, his eyes opened. He was alive! A tidal wave of relief ran through me as I watched him sit up and slowly shake his head.

'Nigel, I'm so sorry, I didn't realize, I must have flicked the wrong switch by mistake,' I babbled as, with a dazed expression, he slowly got to his feet. No response. Had he been struck deaf? 'Nigel, I'm really sorry, are you OK, shall I ring an ambulance?' At that suggestion, he raised his eyebrows. Well, I guess that was progress. He then casually placed his tobacco tin on my kitchen worktop, and without a word, calmly licked the gummy side of the licorice paper and made himself a roll-up. He then flipped open his silver Zippo lighter, lit it and breathed in deeply, sighing as he exhaled the smoke. Finally, he spoke. 'Well, that was fun,' he said. 'See you Monday, Jo.'

As I cooked myself my first decent meal in weeks that evening — having finished the job myself — waves of relief flooded through me. If I already knew one thing about firemen, it was that they were tough. But they also had a wicked sense of humour, and something told me this wouldn't be the last I'd be hearing about this little episode.

★　★　★

'Good morning, gentlemen and Dangerous Jo,' said Nigel breezily as he entered the appliance room for Monday morning roll call.

'Morning, Sub,' we chorused in reply.

'OK, let's get started. Ronnie and Dangerous, can you check the oil, water and wheels on the pump, and all the equipment? When you've finished that little lot, I'll see you in the mess room for coffee. That is, if Ronnie survives that long.' As we set to work and Ronnie quizzed me on what Nigel was talking about, I felt a spring in my step. OK, so I'd narrowly avoided electrocuting the boss, but all in all, things were going well. I'd had a

141

sensible couple of days, eating healthily and going through my cardboard box of belongings.

Among them I'd found a photo of my dad in uniform dated 13 November 1963. As I gazed at his handsome face looking back at me from the sepia image, I felt a massive surge of pride. What with all the upheaval of leaving The Laurels and starting at Thetford, I'd almost forgotten that he'd been an airport fireman. Before I'd joined up, we'd spent countless hours in the kitchen at Eastern Road as he taught me how to press my black wool trousers. 'Always use a sheet of brown paper between the hot plate of the iron and the fabric,' he would explain patiently. 'That way you'll always get a perfect crease at the front.'

I'd loved these lessons, and was completely lost in a daydream about our happy times together when the emergency red phone in the watch room — the front office where Nigel was based — started to ring. As Nigel picked it up and listened intently, we waited wordlessly for our orders. The light-hearted mood of seconds earlier had vanished completely. 'Thetford 1, let's go, it's an RTA, persons reported trapped, on the Mundford Road. MOVE!' he shouted as the alarm bell started to ring.

At last! It was the sound I'd been waiting for ever since I'd started my training — my first daytime shout.

★ ★ ★

In seconds the station was engulfed in a storm of noise, the sheet-metal thunder of the pump bay's roller doors sending an adrenalin rush of fear, intensity and excitement shooting through my system. As Ronnie and I were the closest to the pump, we grabbed our kit and jumped into the two back seats. With Nigel in the front passenger seat and Frank White driving, we were soon hurtling towards our destination. Time seemed to accelerate as we sped past Thetford Rugby Club and headed out of town.

I'd been told there would be days like these, where one minute everything's normal and the next you're thrown into the no man's land between life and death, but nothing can prepare you for when it happens. 'Right, miss,' said Ronnie, sensing my mood. 'Just remember everything that you learned during your training, and you'll be fine. Wait for Nigel to give you your instructions — don't let him out of your sight. And whatever you do, don't get distracted.'

Then I saw it. A beautiful black BMW had

slammed straight into a large oak tree. As we screeched to a halt, I saw thick black rubber tyre marks on the tarmac. The bonnet of the BMW had concertinaed on impact, and I could see the driver was still inside the tangled mass of chrome and black metal. Every fibre of me wanted to run over and help, but I knew it was Nigel's job to assess the situation and make some quick decisions before we did anything. Normally, the first job would be to remove the car battery, but the car had hit the tree with such force the engine block had been pushed backwards, pinning the driver to his seat and making the driver's door inaccessible.

'OK, Jo, I want you to check on the condition of the driver and report straight back to me,' said Nigel. 'Is that understood?' 'Yes, Sub.' As I heaved open the passenger door, I caught my breath. The figure slumped over the wheel looked exactly like Mel Gibson. Blond, twenty-five and dressed in a pinstripe suit with a chunky gold Rolex on his wrist, he had the look of a high-flying sales rep. Automatically, my first-aid training kicked in and I gently lifted his arm from the steering wheel and felt for a pulse. Nothing. But he was still warm. Perhaps he'd just been knocked unconscious? He didn't seem to be bleeding. I checked his pulse again. Nothing.

And again. Nothing.

It was too late. As I slumped back in the passenger seat, a thousand thoughts ran through my mind. Was this man about to impress his boss with some record-breaking sales figures? Or going home to his wife and kids? Or to the pub with his mates? I was shaken from my thoughts by a firm hand on my shoulder. It was Nigel.

'It's too late, there's nothing we can do,' I said calmly when he asked me to check the man's pulse again. 'Looks like he was killed the second he hit the tree.'

He nodded. 'OK, Jo. Let's secure the area and wait for the undertaker to arrive.'

★　★　★

Back at the station, after we'd cleaned up, we gathered in the mess room for a debrief. I must have looked downcast, because as I wheeled my bicycle out of the bike shed afterwards in preparation for the journey home, I saw Mary the cook running out to see me. 'Don't worry, love, they tell me it gets easier,' she said with a gentle smile.

As I pedalled home the streetlights blinked into life and my thoughts began to wander again. Back home, I was replaying the day's events in my head as I sat watching television, still in my work uniform, when I heard a loud knock on the door. Who could it be? I didn't have a single friend in Thetford, and if work wanted me they'd use the house phone. I really wasn't in the mood to see anyone. Whoever it is, I thought, as I roused myself from the sofa, I'm not interested.

To my surprise, I saw two girls of around my age standing on the doorstep. One was wearing a cheesecloth blouse and a long hippy skirt; the other had on stripy jeans and a colourful baggy jumper. 'I know this sounds a bit weird, but could you open this bottle for us, please?' said the taller of the two, thrusting a sealed wine bottle and a corkscrew at me.

'Sure,' I replied. I opened the bottle easily. It must have been all that strength training. 'Thanks so much!' they both trilled, before promptly disappearing into the night. 'Bye!' What was that all about? The truth was, I was too exhausted to care, and I was asleep the second my head hit the pillow.

11

Making Plans for Nigel

'Sub, are you sure this is a good idea?'

It was my first Saturday night out with my new work colleagues and I was beginning to wish I'd stayed at home. I was standing outside the village hall in East Wretham where, judging by the flashing disco lights and the throb of the Bee Gees' 'Stayin' Alive', a raucous party was in full swing.

After my lonely nights at The Dolphin, it seemed like the perfect opportunity to make new friends. But there was one small snag. Instead of my best party dress, I was wearing a full-body furry elephant jumpsuit, complete with large floppy ears and a long grey trunk. There was no two ways about it — I looked bloody ridiculous.

'It's a fancy dress party, lighten up!' boomed Nigel, fastening the zip on an identical outfit that was struggling to contain his muscular six-foot frame. Well, I thought, at least he looks even more stupid than me. 'And for God's sake, stop calling me Sub. We're not at work now. It's time to have some fun, Firefighter Reynolds. That's an order.'

★   ★   ★

Ever since my first daytime shout, my relationship with my workmates had undergone a transformation. It was like the flicking of a switch. One minute I was the new girl who everyone tiptoed around. The next, I was a fully fledged member of the team for whom no practical joke was deemed too cruel or humiliating.

The ringleaders in this campaign of light-hearted terror were Trevor Leggett and another slightly older fireman called Robbie Knowles. Trevor was about my age, and while he was happily married to Debbie, a nurse, we had instantly clicked. 'We get on like a house on fire, don't we, Jo?' he'd say, making me drop my guard for a second before he and Robbie lifted me up and dunked me in the water tank in the corner of the drill yard. 'That should cool things down a bit.'

Other times I would be happily going about my duties when, after hearing a creaking door or some muffled laughter, a strategically placed bucket of iced water would land on my head, soaking me to the skin. 'YOU BLOODY BASTARDS! I'll get you for this!' I'd yell, shaking with rage or laughter depending on how many times that day I'd already had to change out of my sopping wet kit.

Some people might have lost their temper on being subjected to such humiliations. But I saw them for exactly what they were — proof that I had been accepted as a member of the crew.

* * *

The invitation had arrived the previous week. 'Do you fancy a night out with us old timers, Dangerous?' said Nigel, thrusting a multicoloured flyer for a 'Gnomes and Elves' fancy dress party into my hands. 'It's from our friends at the police station across the road. Their parties are legendarily good. And it'll be a chance for you to meet some new people to electrocute.'

'Sounds good to me,' I replied, examining the flyer. 'But where on earth are we going to get the gnome outfits from?'

'I know just the place,' he said.

Twenty minutes later I was standing at the counter of a down-at-heel tattoo parlour on the other side of Thetford. After five minutes, a teenage assistant emerged from the back room munching on a ham roll. When he caught sight of the imposing figure standing in front of him, the blood drained from his face.

'Don't worry, son, I'm not here to check these premises comply with fire department regulations,' he boomed, sensing the boy's anxiety. 'I'm sure they meet the required standards. I'm actually here looking for gnomes.'

'Eh?'

'Gnomes. You do stock fancy dress here as well as cover people's bodies in ink, don't you?'

'Y-y-yes we do,' he stuttered, a look of relief etched on his features. 'But I'm afraid we're all out of gnomes. And elves for that matter. Someone came down here from the police station and took the lot. The only thing we've got that's vaguely similar is a pair of elephant outfits. You can have them if you like.'

Nigel looked at me, then back at the assistant.

'Elephants it is, then.'

★ ★ ★

'I think you'll find Kilverstone Zoo is that way,' said a man standing in the doorway dressed as Robin Hood. 'This party is for gnomes and elves only.' I recognized him as David Barton, a policeman I'd met at the early morning incident with the hay baler, and was relieved to see a broad smile on his face. 'Well, seeing as it's you two, I suppose I can make an exception,' he said, once Nigel had explained away our sartorial shortcomings. 'Into the grotto you go . . . '

As I walked into the hall, I immediately felt immersed in a cocoon of friendliness and warmth. Even from my own limited experience, I knew instinctively that this was how a party ought to be. Unlike the few dreary student bashes I'd been to, where the boys clung nervously to the walls and the girls swayed dolefully to The Smiths, this was a thoroughly adult affair. These people liked and trusted each other, and after a tough week at work were determined to have a good time. As Nigel introduced me to various people, I found myself chatting away without any feeling of awkwardness.

It was already the best party I'd ever been to when I met Chris. He was wearing a samurai outfit, which instantly endeared him to me, standing off to the side of a knot of elves animatedly talking about the new traffic lights on Mundford Road.

His dark hair, broad shoulders and kind eyes said 'strong and intelligent' rather than 'macho and egotistical' and I found myself hovering on the edge of the group, feigning interest just to be near to him. He caught my eye and smiled shyly. *Save me*, he mouthed.

'Hello, you must be the elephant in the room,' he said after I'd walked right over to him. 'That's me,' I croaked, frustrated at my inability to respond with an equally witty one-liner. Thankfully, he didn't seem put off by this lame response, and his grin turned into a dazzling smile when I explained I'd started working at Thetford as a firefighter. 'I've heard of equal opportunities but that's taking things a bit far, isn't it?' he said, motioning to my oversized grey ears. 'Still, I guess my views are irrelevant. Or even irrelephant. Fancy a refill?'

I laughed, and realized I was blushing. What was it about this guy? As he headed to the bar, casting me a quick backwards glance, I seized the opportunity to give him a hasty once-over. Beneath the oblong-shaped folds of his samurai outfit I could see he was tall and lean, muscular without looking like he spent all his spare time in the gym. It was his eyes that really grabbed my attention, though. Cool green pools of light, they seemed to say, this man is at peace with the world.

As we got talking, I felt more at ease than I had with anyone since my teenage crush on Rupert at the country house hotel. But this was different. Whereas most guys engaged me in flirtatious chit-chat, Chris wanted to talk properly about life, the universe, everything. He was confident without being arrogant; thoughtful without being a drip. He explained that he had grown up in Scotland and that he'd moved to Norfolk to be near his parents who had retired here.

As we chatted about our interests, he explained that his samurai outfit wasn't just to stand out from the crowd. He had a deep interest in history, and ran his own antique shop in town. Unlike the many reporters who had asked me the same question many times in recent months, when he asked me why I had wanted to be a firefighter I could tell he wasn't just making small talk — he genuinely wanted to know. I found myself talking about the photo I'd found of my dad, and how he'd been a fireman, too. 'So you're following in the family tradition,' he said thoughtfully. 'That's really admirable. Although it sounds to me like you could turn your hand to anything.'

From anyone else, this would have sounded cheesy. But from Chris it just sounded encouraging. We were still deep in conversation as the lights went up. 'Gnome time, I guess,' he said as we stood outside, both of us giggling like school kids as we watched the last stragglers wearily making their way home in their green and red costumes. As we said goodnight, he took my hand a second longer than was necessary, and our eyes locked in a way that told me we'd be seeing each other again. Was it just the booze making me feel so light-headed?

In the taxi back to Thetford with Nigel, I wound down the window and gulped down heady blasts of cool night air. 'Erm, Nigel do you know anything about that guy Chris?' I asked as casually as possible, as we sped our way through the dark country lanes. 'I thought you'd never ask,' he said, his elephant costume now unfastened to his chest, and a licorice roll-up between his lips. 'He's a Womble.'

'What do you mean?' I said, as images of Uncle Bulgaria and Madame Cholet swam through my mind. 'A Womble. That's what we call the retained firefighters. Don't ask me why. Anyway, he's stationed at Thetford. I'm surprised you haven't bumped into him already.'

My heart was beating faster than ever. Not only had I met the man of my dreams, he worked at the same place as me! Maybe this really was fate. As I collapsed into bed, still wearing my elephant outfit, I replayed the whole evening in my head. On reflection, my night out had been a very good idea indeed.

'Really sorry to bother you, but I think we met the other night.' I was sitting alone in The Dolphin, daydreaming about the events of the weekend, when a friendly voice interrupted my thoughts. 'My name's Kay . . . and this is my best friend Sam.' Before I could say a word, the two of them had sat down on either side of me. As they did so, I felt my own energy levels shoot up. They both had brown permed hair and spoke in a fizzy rhythmic banter, firing off funny one-liners to each other as if they were in a sitcom. Whatever gang they were in, I wanted to be a part of it.

It turned out that Sam was the girlfriend of my next door neighbour, Andy. She explained that the pair of them had seen me drinking by myself in The Dolphin, but couldn't quite figure me out. 'Everyone's been talking about you, you know,' said Kay, giving me a friendly nudge. 'They can't tell if you're a boy or a girl, gay or straight.' I'd already guessed that tongues had been wagging, but it was still nice to have my suspicions confirmed. 'So anyway,' continued Sam, 'when we couldn't open the bottle of wine it seemed like the perfect excuse to come and say hello. Because who else do you go to in an emergency but a fireman? I mean, a firewoman . . . '

I'd forgotten how much I missed girly conversation, and these two were clearly past masters at it. It was intoxicating just being with them, and we spent the rest of the evening gossiping away like old friends. After I'd bored them with the details of my long journey from Wales via Wymondham, they told me about their lives. Kay worked in an office at the Travenol factory on the edge of town, while Sam was at secretarial college in Norwich. They were both bright-eyed and curious about life, and I felt an instant connection with them. And judging by the way they knocked back their drinks, it was obvious that if anyone in Thetford knew where the party was, it was these two.

As I got ready for work the next morning, I felt more like my old self. It was June, and it wasn't just the weather that was improving. Not only had I met a mysterious new guy, I'd also, by some small miracle, made a couple of new friends. If only I wasn't so bloody tired. For the past week, I'd been working flat out. A spell of hot weather had left the heathland surrounding Thetford completely starved of water. As we drove back and forth across the county visiting local businesses, it was shocking to see. Miles of normally luscious green scenery had been scorched brown, and the forest was now as dry as a tinderbox.

'Listen up, you lot,' Nigel had said a week earlier, holding up a fax he'd just received from the Forestry Commission. 'This is what is called an 'early warning of wild fires' alert. They are only issued when there is a very high fire risk and it is not to be taken lightly. As you all know, we have the largest lowland pine forest in Europe on our doorstep. However, if one idiot who has gone in there for a picnic or to sunbathe drops a cigarette, right now the whole bloody lot could go up quicker than you can say Jack Robinson. So the Forestry Commission have arranged for a fire duty officer to be on call as well as putting water tanker drivers on standby who can transport emergency 1,000-gallon containers any time, day or night. Now, obviously we're all hoping these won't be needed. But I've seen these conditions before, and I guarantee we are going to be very busy in the next couple of weeks, so keep your wits about you.'

The first call-out had come in less than half an hour later. From that point on, we'd been putting out small grass fires practically non-stop. For seven whole days, I'd barely washed or changed my clothes, and I'd barely had four hours sleep when the noise I'd begun to hate started up again. *Beep. Beep.*

Beep. 'Bollocks,' I said quietly to myself, picking up a slice of cold toast from the worktop, as I grabbed my keys and hopped on my bike. As I cycled up the road, munching my toast as I went, I realized I wasn't going as fast as usual. The truth was, I didn't want to. I was shattered. All I wanted to do was go home, crawl into bed and sleep. When I turned the corner, my heart sank still further. My dream scenario would have been seeing the pump whizzing past as I feigned disappointment at not making it in time. Instead, the bloody pump was still there, revving its engine with its doors open.

Once again I was left with no choice but to skid to a halt, hurl my bike down against the grass bank, grab my kit, and clamber up into the back seat. I was out of breath, tired, hungry and grumpy, and to make matters worse, I'd got the worst seat on the pump, wedged in the middle of the back row. Thankfully, Ronnie was sitting next to me in his favourite window seat. And judging by the smile on his face he was a lot happier to be there than I was. 'Welcome aboard, Miss Reynolds, we are honoured that you could join us,' he said, shooting me a grin. 'Did you have to come from another county?'

'It's all right for you, Ronnie,' I replied

once we'd got under way and our conversation wasn't audible to the rest of the crew. 'You and the rest of the blokes have always got a hot dinner waiting for you when you get home, and someone cooking you breakfast in the morning. All that's waiting for me is a tin of Co-op marrowfat peas.' Just as he was about to reply, a wail of sirens ripped through our conversational bubble. We'd arrived on the outskirts of a pretty village called Brandon. Or at least, what was left of it.

From every direction, firemen were running around laying hoses as an enormous fire raged at the edge of the woods. This was on a completely different scale to anything I'd seen so far. It felt like I'd walked onto the set of a disaster movie, and I was half expecting a charred-looking Arnold Schwarzenegger to appear when I heard Station Officer Frank Lane barking out his orders. 'Jo and Ronnie — get two others and take the featherweight pump onto the grass verge on the other side of the river, and use water from there,' he said as thick clouds of black smoke snaked into the sky. 'We're going to have to fight this fire by hand. We'll beat down the ground in front of it as much as we can so we can get you as near as possible. It's going to be bloody hot and visibility is going to be virtually non-existent, so for God's sake keep talking

159

to us. A fire like this can go faster than people can run, so whatever you do, don't get cut off.'

As quickly as we could, we lifted the portable pump into place over a makeshift bridge and set off uphill towards the river. As we got closer to the bank I could see we were only part of a huge operation. Over 35 acres of trees, peat and undergrowth had been sucked into the blaze and the scorched grassland in front of us looked like something out of *Apocalypse Now*. There were isolated fires burning all around us as well as ominous-looking piles of still smouldering ash, and I could see crews from five pumps from across Norfolk and Suffolk at work, damping down fires and trying to prevent new ones.

With two guys working the pump, Ronnie and I took up position. The bone-dry grass crunched under my feet like straw, and as sparks flew out from the blaze I felt a shiver run down my spine. The golden rule of firefighting was always to remain upwind of any blaze, but I knew that if a thermal scattered some sparks behind us, we could be in serious trouble. 'Keep calm, Jo, you're doing a great job,' I heard Ronnie shout from behind me, perhaps sensing how nervous I was. 'Stick to what you're doing and we'll be fine.'

Locking the hose under my right arm and aiming the nozzle into the heart of the blaze, I felt all those months of training paying off. As we inched forwards, I felt even better than I had during the airport fire. This was the real thing! Was there any feeling on earth better than facing down a fire head-on, and winning?

After four hours we had a food break. On a shout of 'Grub's up!' vast tureens of stew, potatoes and baked beans appeared as if by magic, which were then heated and put into one huge mixing pot. Anything would have tasted delicious at that point, but as Ronnie and I tucked in, sitting on a tinder-dry grass bank, it tasted like nothing else.

My arms ached like hell, and my t-shirt was soaked through with sweat, but it didn't matter. Seeing my colleagues still hard at work around me, fighting the blaze as sparks fizzed and popped in the crimson sky, I was almost overcome with emotion. I'd never felt more warmth for my fellow man.

'Well . . . it is bloody boiling here,' said Ronnie with a grin when I said as much. 'Personally, I think that's your stomach talking. It's telling you to stay here and not go home to your tin of marrowfat peas!'

After we'd finally packed away our kit,

ensuring that all the hoses were completely drained, the storage racks on the pump were full and no one had 'accidentally' taken any of our equipment, we headed back to the station. As I cycled back to the cottage at 8 p.m., all I could think about was crawling into bed.

Until, that is, I found a note attached to my front door.

Hey Jo
Heard you've been busy. Sounds like thirsty work.
We're at The Central Hotel if you fancy a drink?
Love
Kay & Sam

I was exhausted. But I was even more tired of never having any time off. In ten minutes flat, I'd dug out my one party dress, put on some lipstick and was slamming the door shut behind me. It was time to have some fun.

12

Suspect Device

It was 11.15 on a quiet Friday morning and I was under attack. Trevor and I had just finished scrubbing both fire engines to a Mr Sheen-worthy gleam, and were now playing our favourite game: 'Sponge'. This involved hurling soaking wet sponges at each other in the yard, just outside the pump bay.

Thwack! I heard the sub-atomic whoosh as a watery missile whizzed past my left ear and thudded against the wall behind me. *Splat!* A second projectile hit the wheel arch I was crouching behind, spraying me with freezing cold, soapy water. I was about to unleash my own soggy version of Armageddon when I heard Ronnie shouting to us from the mess room. 'Oi, you two, stop messing about and come in here and take a look at this!'

I walked into the mess room to find everyone crowded around the television. 'What's all the fuss about?' I said, wedging myself closer to get a better look.

'The IRA have only gone and blown up the entire Tory cabinet,' said Ronnie, shaking his head in disbelief. I stared at the screen, almost unable to take it in. A bomb had ripped apart the front section of the Grand Hotel in Brighton, killing five people and sending masonry crashing down on guests sleeping in the rooms below.

As firefighters helped ashen-faced victims escape from the wreckage, a detective explained that a bomb had been detonated using a slow release mechanism. My blood ran cold. Only the previous week we'd had a talk from a steely-eyed officer from the bomb disposal unit based at RAF Wittering in Cambridgeshire.

Although it had been a routine visit, we were acutely aware that Thetford held a unique position in terms of military importance. Situated 7 miles north of town was the Stanford Battle Area. A vast military base spanning 30,000 acres, it was an obvious terrorist target and right in the middle of our patch. It had also been where they'd filmed the tide sequence for *Dad's Army*, although it had been clear from the officer's demeanour that his subject was no laughing matter.

'I'm here to talk to you about Improvised Explosive Devices, or IEDs.' His tone, his expression, *those eyes* — everything about this guy said he meant business. 'We have evidence that the IRA, in particular, are moving towards creating bombs of increased sophistication,' he continued. 'A lot of these devices are very easy to make and can be constructed from everyday household items. You need to know what they look like, which is why I've brought one along with me . . . ' From out of a leather satchel, he pulled a cardboard box not much bigger than a cigarette packet. Inside it was a spring-loaded clothes peg. A small wire led from each of its jaws to two 1.5 volt batteries connected to a small plastic envelope filled with sugar and chloral hydrate.

'As you can see, it also has a rudimentary delay mechanism,' he said, pointing to a length of lead soldering wire wrapped around the jaws of the clothes peg. 'When the wire gets stretched, the circuit becomes closed, igniting the incendiary mixture and producing a brief, but intense, fireball. We believe devices like these may soon be used on, shall we say, sensitive targets.' Both his visit and the news of the IRA bomb were salutary reminders of quite how serious our job could be, as I was about to find out.

★ ★ ★

The call came in later that afternoon. A bedroom fire had been reported in Lincoln

Way, on Thetford's most notorious housing estate, Abbey Farm.

'Scabby Farm, here we come!' said Ronnie sarcastically as we squeezed into our usual seats on the back row of the pump. I had to laugh. Call-outs to this estate always came with complications. Even since I'd started we'd had countless false alarms when mischievous, or just plain bored, kids had dialled 999, only to deny all knowledge when we got there. 'OK then, sonny, let's press redial on your home phone, shall we?' Nigel would say patiently, as the supposed 'fire' turned out to be yet another hoax.

As we pulled up outside a scruffy-looking street of terraced houses I could see that at least this one was genuine. Smoke was billowing from an upstairs window and although it was a 'no persons reported', meaning no one was in the house, the fire still had to be extinguished as quickly as possible.

While Nigel talked to the neighbours to find out what was going on, Trevor and I plus two of our retained colleagues dropped the ladder from the back of the pump and under-ran it to beneath the bedroom window. On Nigel's signal, we both hot-footed it up the ladder to the first-floor window ledge with me at the front carrying the hose reel.

It was only when I pushed open the

window that the world tipped sideways. An ear-splitting noise — like a bomb going off — sent the air rushing out of my lungs. A split second later, I was clinging to the ladder and struggling to breathe as a sensory overload — double vision, nausea, chest pain — hit me. I'd also, I realized to my horror, been struck deaf. 'What the fuck was that?!' I shouted down to Trevor, unable to hear myself speak. He looked almost as shaken from the blast as me, and I could just about read his lips. 'I think it must have been a flashover.'

A flashover! These were the stuff of legend, the kind of thing usually reserved for Hollywood movies and the anecdotes of grizzled 'smoke-eaters'. They were also the firefighter's worst nightmare, occurring when the combination of fire and gases in a room caused every combustible to ignite at once.

'Jo! Stop dithering about and put this bloody fire out!' I heard Nigel shout from below, alerting me to the fact we still had a job to do. Well, I thought to myself, at least I'm not deaf any more.

Once the blaze was extinguished, and still slightly dazed, I stood with Trevor on the small concrete patio at the front of the house. A red plastic kid's trike sat abandoned on a nearby drive, a couple of skinheads were tinkering with a stripped-back Lambretta in the front garden opposite, and Frankie Goes to Hollywood's 'Two Tribes' was blaring from a car radio.

To all intents and purposes, it was another normal day on Abbey Farm. And yet, we'd just experienced a flashover. It was hard to take in. 'Right,' said Nigel, coming over to see us. 'I expect you two are wondering what just happened up there.' I was still unsteady on my feet and the waft of his licorice cigarette, for once, felt strangely comforting. 'Well, let me enlighten you. I've just spoken to the mother of the boy whose bedroom was on fire. It turns out that he's been stockpiling munitions. She tells me he found them at The Nunnery, which was the Home Guard's base back in World War Two. Anyway, in among them was a whole load of what were called 'sticky bombs' back in the day. These were anti-tank grenades packed with nitroglycerin, which have been left lying about for the last forty years.'

He took a last draw on his cigarette and ground it out with a deliberate corkscrewing movement. 'By opening that window and letting oxygen in, you blew the whole lot up. Dangerous, you're lucky to be alive.'

It was on the journey back to the station that the jokes started up. 'Well, it doesn't get any more *Dad's Army* than that,' said Trevor with a grin, clearly now fully recovered. 'A bedroom full of hand grenades, an explosion and the Home Guard. The only thing missing was Mr Mainwaring.' Without missing a beat, he went into his best impersonation of Lance Corporal Jones. 'Don't panic, Mr Mainwaring, don't panic!' he bellowed as everyone on the pump roared with laughter. 'Jo is here to save us!' I poked my tongue out at him and tried desperately not to laugh. Just wait until our next game of 'Sponge', I said to myself. You'll be sorry.

⋆ ⋆ ⋆

'You've got a bottom just like a boy,' said a camp voice behind me. I was walking up the stairs of The Central Hotel with a glass of cider in my hand and I knew it could only be one person, Keith, the pub's co-owner.

It had been nearly a month since I'd almost had my ears perforated by the flashover and my social life, I was delighted to say, had improved dramatically. Thanks to Kay and Sam, who I quickly discovered knew *everybody*, I was now part of a lively social circle centred around Thetford Rugby Club. Christmas was around the corner, and being part of this new gang felt exhilarating after all my solitary nights at The Dolphin.

I'd also decided to forget about Chris. Or at least, put him to the back of my mind. I hadn't seen him at any of my call-outs at Thetford, and I'd heard on the grapevine that he had a steady girlfriend called Nicky. She was a policewoman who worked at the station that was literally across the road from us. The more I thought about this, the more confusing it seemed. Why had I not seen them together? Either at her workplace or mine? And where had she been hiding at the 'Gnomes and Elves' party? Under a toadstool?

Partially because of this news, I'd hooked up with a friend of Kay and Sam's called Paul. I wanted some uncomplicated fun, and he fitted the bill perfectly.

Slim, dark-haired and easygoing, Paul lived with his parents in a detached house close to the river. Usually dressed in an open-necked shirt, leather bomber jacket and jeans, his main passions were judo, cars and his family. Paul's nickname for me was 'Sexy Legs', which I found a refreshing change from the usual 'Are you a man or a woman?' remarks I'd receive while out and about in town with my colleagues. On Saturday afternoons, Paul played rugby for Thetford, and I became a regular at the club's ground, cheering him from the sidelines alongside Kay, Sam and the rest of the 'rugby girlfriends' before we all trooped back to The Central Hotel.

A former coaching inn on the town's market square, the pub was run by an extravagant gay couple called Mike and Keith. I'd thought the fire service guys were larger than life, but they had nothing on these two. Mike was a mild-mannered former rugby player who thought it was perfectly OK to serve customers their lunchtime scampi and chips wearing a tight black t-shirt, leather trousers and a black leather cap with a silver chain.

Keith was even more flamboyant. Tall and lean with a bleached blond mullet, he always wore the same outfit — a Persil white t-shirt, skin-tight stonewash jeans and white trainers, even when preparing food in the kitchen. Keith saw himself as an artist. Anyone foolish enough to ask for their steak well done or — heaven forbid — for tomato sauce to be brought to their table would risk igniting the kind of explosion not seen since Krakatoa.

'Tell them, if they don't like it they can fuck off!' he would scream when such impossible demands were relayed to the kitchen. 'These fucking peasants don't deserve to eat my food!'

At this point Mike would excuse himself

from behind the bar, and, gently taking his arm, escort the hysterical chef upstairs. Moments later the soothing sounds of Edith Piaf singing 'Non, Je Ne Regrette Rien' would reverberate through the floorboards, as Keith's despair at mankind's stupidity was temporarily abated. Luckily for me, Mike and Keith loved all the firefighters at Thetford, and I was soon part of their inner circle.

* * *

It had been a typical Friday evening spent with Paul and the rest of the gang: Kay, Sam, other friends Helen and Linnie and various rugby-playing mates of Paul's. As usual Keith and Mike had insisted on a lock-in after the pub closed, and I was upstairs in their messy 'den', part of their private apartment on the third floor.

It was the kind of lived-in front room I craved for myself. A dark red sofa — the kind you can lose yourself in — was wedged against one wall in front of a solid oak coffee table, which was strewn with half-empty wine glasses and an overflowing ashtray. There were records everywhere, cigarette burns on the tasteful Afghan rug and large sash windows on two sides that afforded a bird's-eye view of Thetford's main square.

'I'll make us something to forget it's bloody Christmas,' said Keith, sitting down to roll one of his perfectly constructed joints as the opening bars of Grace Jones's 'Slave to the Rhythm' crackled from the speakers. As I danced around the room, I felt a lightness I hadn't felt in years. This is where I ought to be, I told myself, as Grace serenaded me. At least for now.

'Look at those little bastards!' said Keith, breaking the spell. I picked up my glass of cider from the table and joined him at the window. A drunken argument had broken out between two groups of lads wearing matching red Father Christmas bobble hats. We both watched impassively as it escalated into the inevitable Friday night punch-up. 'It's no wonder I smoke this stuff,' said Keith, taking a deep hit before passing me the joint. 'Their parents should have been sterilized at birth.' He laughed mirthlessly. 'Tell you what, someone get a needle, and I'll go out there and sterilize these bastards now. That'll be a Christmas present they won't forget!'

I took a long toke and felt a calmness sweep through me as the sweet smoke filled my lungs. Unwinding with Keith and the gang was just what I needed. It had been a long week. High winds had been causing havoc, and among countless minor incidents caused by fallen trees, there had been a particularly nasty one.

We'd been called out to the RAF base at Barnham, a couple of miles out of town, on the edge of Thetford Heath. As we got closer we could see a beige Austin Maxi that had been stopped in its tracks. A large tree branch had been blown down by a gust of wind at precisely the moment the car was driving past. It had crashed straight through the front windscreen and killed the driver instantly. It was a gruesome sight. The branch had hit the car sideways on, and ended up in the man's mouth. Alfred Hitchcock couldn't have come up with anything more horrific. We'd had to wait for the doctor to certify the poor man dead, and the car had needed to be cut apart to extract him — it had taken hours.

'I don't know, Keith, life sometimes seems so . . . pointless,' I said, exhaling as I watched the knuckleheads below slug it out. 'People's lives are ruined by freak accidents every day and their loved ones are just expected to get on with it. There's no rhyme or reason to any of it.' I felt the marijuana coursing through my system, sending my imagination into overdrive. An image of Neil Dallas flashed through my mind. Then the young guy impaled on the hay baler, now the poor guy in the Austin Maxi. Would the face of every dead person I saw end up being etched indelibly on my memory?

'Well, the way I look at it, we've all got to go at some point, darling,' replied Keith, puncturing my maudlin mood. 'So you may as well go out in style.'

As I laughed, I felt someone squeezing me around the waist from behind. 'Hello Sexy Legs, I thought I'd find you up here,' said Paul, his arms entwined around my body as he nuzzled my neck. 'I'm off home, I've got a match tomorrow. See you there, yeah?'

'OK, great, see you then.' As Paul's footsteps descended the stairs, Keith raised his empty glass. 'One for the road?'

★　★　★

I'd always hated New Year's Eve. There was too much pressure to have a good time, too many 'fun' things that had to happen to make it a success (a decent party to go to, the corny countdown to midnight, the — ugh — singing of 'Auld Lang Syne' when the clock struck twelve). However, even I was feeling a tingle of anticipation as I got ready for the big bash at The Central Hotel. The whole place had been done out in festive red, white and green bunting, and we'd been instructed firmly by Keith and Mike that it was a strict fancy dress code — no one would be allowed in wearing what Keith called 'civilian' clothes.

I'd decided to push the boat out, and chosen to dress up in a 1920s Charleston outfit. I'd acquired some pearls, feathers, black stockings and a sparkly black Flapper dress, and felt more feminine than I had in years as I got ready for the big night.

'Tonight you're going to be chic, elegant and sophisticated,' I said to myself, admiring my reflection in the mirror. I just hoped Paul was going to be sporting something equally classy. He hadn't told me what he was going to wear, promising that it would be 'a surprise'.

At that moment, there was a ring on the doorbell. When I opened it, I almost had a heart attack. I was face to face with a 7-foot tall, bright orange fuzzy bear. It was Paul, dressed as the Honey Monster. 'It's all about the honey, mummy,' he said.

It was a party so good, no one would remember a thing about it. It felt like everyone I'd ever met from the fire station, the rugby club or just out and about in town was there, and they were all resolute in their determination to have a good time.

As the party wound on, I found myself sitting with Nigel, and a few of the others from the station. I enjoyed hanging out with the rugby crowd, but there was something about these men that set them apart. Not only were they upstanding members of society, they really knew how to enjoy themselves.

For some reason best known to himself, Nigel had come as an American football player. A silver grid-iron helmet sat on the table in front of him and his giant frame was cased in a blue nylon shirt that even had his name on the back. 'You know what, Mr Monument, I really, really love my job,' I said, punching him affectionately on the shoulder pad. I'd had five glasses of wine, two gin and tonics and three peach schnapps and vodka already, and the room was starting to spin.

'Whoa, come on, Jo, it's a bit early to get sentimental,' he boomed in reply. 'It's still five minutes to midnight.'

'You're right,' I slurred, slumping even further in my seat. 'Let's talk about something else.'

'All right then,' he replied. 'Did you know I could fly?'

'What?' I said, not really knowing what he was talking about. 'Do go on.'

'Well, I haven't got my licence yet but I've been taking lessons with a mate of mine who also flies vintage planes on open days at the airfield. Last week I went up with him in a

1930s Tiger Moth. When we got to the right altitude, he passed me a hessian bag full of rolls of pink toilet paper and told me to throw them out of the cockpit like streamers. Then he flew straight through them, cutting them to pieces. It was like the sky was full of pink confetti — the crowd loved it.'

I was still marvelling at this mental image when something caught my eye. Through the mingling crowds, I could see a man at the bar dressed as a samurai warrior. It was Chris. My heart skipped a beat. 'Sorry, Nigel . . . there's someone I need to say hello to,' I said, levering myself up and making my way over to where Chris was standing with his back to me. 'You're a long way from Wimbledon Common, aren't you, Tomsk?' I said, tapping him on the shoulder.

'Sorry?'

'Everyone at the station tells me you're a Womble,' I continued confidently, my usual inhibitions washed away on a tide of alcohol. 'That is where Wombles live, isn't it?' He broke into a smile. *That* smile. It was hard to breathe, everything about him seemed so . . . right. After a few minutes of flirtatious small talk, I decided to cut to the chase.

'So, why didn't you tell me you had a girlfriend?'

'You didn't ask.'

'Well, I didn't ask you about lots of things,' I heard myself saying, just as the music stopped and the countdown to New Year began. Oh god. Just when it was going so well.

'TEN . . . '

'Listen,' he said, leaning closer so I could hear him.

'NINE . . . '

'I'm doing up a house in town . . . '

'EIGHT . . . '

'It's a major project and . . . '

'SEVEN . . . '

'A few of the guys from the station are coming over to help next weekend.'

'SIX . . . '

' . . . to help do it up . . . '

'FIVE . . . '

'I was wondering if you fancied it?'

'FOUR . . . '

'I've also got some lethal home brew to drink . . . '

'THREE . . . '

' . . . if that would help . . . '

'TWO . . . '

' . . . to tempt you?'

'ONE . . . '

He smiled. He smelt of beer, adventure, fun.

'OK then,' I said, looking into his eyes.

'Happy New Year, Tomsk.'

That night as I fell into bed, strange visions filled my dreams. I was in the cockpit of a Tiger Moth being flown by a man dressed as a samurai. I was laughing hysterically as the plane weaved through the clouds, surrounded by pink confetti. Suddenly, the engine stopped. The sky turned black. We were crashing. As I woke up, all I could hear were screams.

13

Highway to Hell

Overnight, it seemed, my life had become one long date with death and disaster. After months of wondering when the action would start, I was suddenly in the thick of it. We'd been to countless call-outs over Christmas and New Year, and as January got under way they showed no sign of letting up.

'Earth to Jo . . . earth to Jo . . . You haven't listened to a word I've said, have you?' said Ronnie, jolting me out of my daydream. We were sitting in the mess room, and my thoughts had clearly started to wander.

'Erm, sorry, Ronnie,' I spluttered, frantically trying to remember what he'd been talking about. Ah yes — how the job had changed over the years.

' . . . I was explaining that when I started we had nothing like the equipment we've got now,' he continued, unaware of quite how far I'd drifted off. 'When you went to a road accident back in those days you had a hammer, a chisel and a hacksaw and that was about it. It was like trying to cut a car open with a tin opener.' I wanted to laugh, but something about the look Ronnie gave me prevented it. 'You just had to do your best and move on to the next one. I've been to motorbike accidents where you're literally picking up body parts as you walk along the road and putting them in a bin bag. A foot here, a knee there, then sweeping the rest down the drain and going home for tea. That's what we do. You just have to try and forget about it.'

I was beginning to realize that these unofficial chats were the crew's way of making sense of the job. Back in the eighties there was no such thing as counselling — for any emergency service personnel. Instead, even the most horrific incidents had to be dealt with, and, if possible, pushed to the back of the mind. 'There'll be plenty more nasty accidents before this winter's over,' he said, almost to himself. 'When the temperature drops, a section of the road surface freezes over at Brandon, about a mile outside Thetford. It's got something to do with the way the wind comes through the forest, but of course, no one driving innocently along there knows that. The road turns into a death trap, waiting for its next victim.' It wouldn't be long before I found that out for myself.

It was a scene from Dante's Inferno. Broken bones and random body parts were strewn across the road. The smell of burning flesh, scorched metal and molten rubber, meanwhile, was sending shockwaves shooting through my nervous system.

It was first thing in the morning, and we'd been called out to the A11 near Attleborough. A woman driver waiting to turn right on the central reservation had been hit from behind by a lorry and pushed into the path of a lorry coming the other way. She'd been sandwiched between them, and incinerated instantly. All that was left of her was a charred carcass, still sitting in the driver's seat. 'Jo, stop gawping, get a shovel and get to work!' barked Nigel, jolting me from my stupor.

As I gently tried to lift the woman's body from the wreckage, I realized it wasn't going to be easy. She had been stuck to the leather car seat by the heat of the fire following the collision. The more I tried to pull her free, the more heart-breaking it became. God, please give me strength, I thought, as I finally managed to place her remains in a body bag as carefully as I possibly could.

As I got down on my hands and knees on the scarred tarmac and shovelled up the rest of the debris, an icy wind picked up. The hot ashes formed a macabre snowstorm around me, clogging my lungs and making me gasp for air. I was fighting back tears, and not just for this poor woman; it was obvious her pet dog, too, had been burned alive.

When I finally got home I was glad to find Paul there waiting for me. We'd been rowing constantly over stupid little things for the last few weeks, but at that moment I was delighted to see him. Paul gave fabulous bear hugs, the kind you never wanted to end. Then he did what any right thinking person would do, and cracked open a bottle of wine. As he handed me a glass and a box of tissues, I realized there were still tiny flecks of dried blood on my clothes. I was still numb with shock. But nowhere near numb enough. I brushed away the tiny dark-red dots, watching as these tiny particles, all that was left of one woman's hopes and dreams, vanished into thin air. There was only one thing for it.

'Let's get drunk,' I said, downing my glass of wine in one gulp.

★ ★ ★

I'd been looking forward to seeing Chris, but I was still silently cursing the fact I'd be missing this week's Saturday afternoon film, *Blithe Spirit*, starring Margaret Rutherford, when I saw Kay, Sam and Nigel standing outside his front door on Thetford High Street. It was a bright cold January day, and their combined high spirits quickly shook me out of my grouchy mood. Chris's house was directly opposite The Central Hotel and, knowing Kay and Sam, I was pretty sure we'd end up there afterwards.

As I stepped through the heavy wooden door, I quickly realized this wasn't going to be an 'ask your mates around to slap paint on the walls' kind of event.

A black and white timber-framed Tudor house dating to the 1500s, it was more of a crumbling relic than somewhere to live. I could see that restoring it to its former glory was an immense project. But as he showed us around the interior, pointing out the crown-post roof and pointing to where the original wattle and daub walls had started to come away, I began to see it through Chris's eyes.

It occurred to me that this was also the first time I'd seen him out of his samurai outfit. Dressed in a scruffy V-neck jumper and jeans, he looked a bit like the romantic lead from one of my favourite black and white movies. Then it dawned on me: he looked exactly like Clark Gable, if a bit rougher round the edges.

By mid-afternoon, I was upstairs happily polishing the leaded glass in one of the original casement windows. Sam had brought along her brand new compact disc player, and I was in my own little world, singing along to Squeeze's 'Cool for Cats', when I heard a voice behind me.

'It might not look it, but Thetford is a fascinating place,' said Chris. 'For instance, did you know Boudicca — or Boadicea as they called her in school — was based here during the Iron Age?' I shook my head and gave him my most attentive look. 'Well, as you probably know, she was the Queen of the Iceni tribe, and our greatest warrior queen. You can still see the ramparts of their fortress at Castle Hill, and there are also signs of a settlement at Gallows Hill. The strange thing is, no one knows exactly where or how she died. Some historians think she poisoned herself rather than risk capture, but person-ally, my theory is that — '

At that exact moment a piercing scream come from downstairs. 'What the bloody hell is *that?*' shouted Sam. As we came running down the stairs we could see her pointing at what looked like a pile of ancient rags.

'A-ha, I thought we might find one of these,' said Chris, striding over and gently picking up what appeared to be a dusty bag of bones. 'It's a mummified cat. The Tudors used them as magic charms to ward off evil spirits.'

'Talking of evil spirits . . . ' said Nigel, gesturing towards the open doors of The Central. 'Shall we?'

★　★　★

In the pub, I got to know Chris a little better. Like the other retained firemen he only worked part-time at Thetford. Most of his time was spent running the antique shop below the house, and visiting local auctions. This at least explained why I'd never seen him at the station. 'I mostly go to Diss, you can pick up all sorts there,' he explained, once we'd taken up position at a long wooden table by the window. 'I'm interested in anything and everything really. In the last few weeks I've picked up a pair of flintlock pistols, a Georgian chest of drawers and some Victorian candlesticks.'

I couldn't help but laugh. From what I'd seen through the windows, Chris's shop looked like the archetypal 'Old Curiosity Shop'. There was so much stuff in there you could barely swing a cat — even a mummified one. 'I like anything that's got some history to it, but my real passion are netsuke,' he continued. 'They're miniature sculptures that were used in Japan as buttons on coats — they work in the same way as a toggle on a duffle coat. The earliest examples date back to the seventeenth century, during the Edo period. Sorry, this must be terribly boring for you.'

'No, not at all,' I gushed, urging him to carry on. I hadn't feigned this much enthusiasm since Fanny French's classes at Whitland!

'Anyway, that's enough about my boring obsessions,' he said. 'You strike me as the kind of girl who wants the world and everything in it. What makes your heart beat a little faster?'

Frantically, I made a quick mental note of my current obsessions. Think, Jo, think. Well, I was a great admirer of the work of Cagney and Lacey, New York's finest women cops. As for history, I knew everything there was to know about Alexis Carrington, Joan Collins's character in the hit TV show, Dynasty. But that was about it. 'Oh, I've got a broad range of cultural influences,' I heard myself saying, as he looked at me eagerly. 'But really, don't get me started. We could be here all night . . . '

Thankfully we soon slipped into small talk about fire service personnel we both knew. It had been an enjoyable evening, but I was tired from a long week at work and made my excuses to leave. As I did so, Chris fished in his pocket and pulled out a silver coin the size of a five pence piece.

'I found a load of these in the house the other day,' he said, passing it to me. 'It's a solid silver sixpence, dating to about 1580, so it's about four hundred years old. It's amazing to think how many people must have handled it at one time or another.'

He paused. 'You can have it if you want, for good luck when you're out on shouts.'

What was it with guys and good luck charms? I thought to myself. I still carried everywhere the 'Different Day, Same Shit' badge Graeme had given me. 'Thanks,' I said, turning it over in the palm of my hand before passing it back to him. 'But judging by the state of your place, you're going to need all the luck you can get if the weather turns really cold. I'll probably get called out to save you from dying of hypothermia.'

★ ★ ★

As I cycled back home, I replayed the events of the last few days in my head. I loved my job, but talking to Chris had reminded me there was a whole world out there, waiting to be explored. I knew most of my colleagues were happily settled in Thetford and had no desire to leave. For some of the senior hands, even London was another country, mention of it a cue for a roll of the eyes and grumbles about the attitude of people in 'the smoke'. I genuinely admired these men, but I hated this small town mentality. If I stayed here for the next twenty-five years, would I end up like that?

By the time I got home it was ten o'clock. I was exhausted and all I wanted to do was catch up on some sleep. But as I sat down on the sofa and idly flicked on the TV, I saw that the late film — a slushy biopic of the country star Patsy Cline called *Sweet Dreams* — was about to start. I loved Patsy and, having missed my afternoon movie fix, decided this would have to take its place. I curled up under my favourite blanket, noticing that there was still half a bag of Maltesers wedged down the side of the sofa from the previous weekend. Result!

As I sat in the darkness, I drifted into my own little world. I'd come a long way from my lonely nights watching *Dallas* on the black and white television back at Ben-y-Mar. But perhaps Chris was right; maybe I really did want the world and everything in it.

14

Shock the Monkey

I was eyeball to eyeball with a large and very angry South American monkey. From within a ghostly white face, two blood-red eyes stared directly back at me. *Your move*, they seemed to say. For the past four hours, we'd been chasing this peeved primate across town after a daring escape from Kilverstone Zoo. However, with the Saturday afternoon traffic building up, it had to be recaptured soon if this little bit of monkey business wasn't going to end with her splattered all over the A11. I aimed the hose at the creature's tawny midriff and took a deep breath. What was it that the zookeeper had just told me? 'Be careful — when they're frightened these animals can rip your face clean off with one paw.' Nice. I opened the branch of the hose and let rip. As a high-pressure jet of water flew from the nozzle, the monkey let out an ear-piercing scream.

★   ★   ★

Up until this point, it had been a quiet week. In fact, it had been downright lazy. My bleeper hadn't gone off once, and it felt like the whole of Norfolk was basking under the scorching July heat, its face under a wet towel. Thursday had been another blazing hot afternoon, and I'd decided to make the most of it. I was wearing a flimsy cotton vest, tiny denim shorts and flip-flops, soaking up the sunshine in the garden of The Black Horse with Kay and Sam. 'So give me all the gossip about what happened at Glastonbury then,' I said to Kay as Sam brought over three halves of cider on a tin tray. 'I want to know everything — what bands you saw, how you coped with the mud, and most of all, who you managed to lure back to your tents to have your wicked way with?'

This was a subject that I knew could keep them both talking for days, and I was happy to listen. After all the horrific things I'd had to face over the last few months I was desperate to think about something more frivolous. I also knew Kay and Sam's love lives were as complex as particle string theory, and that any talk of festivals would inevitably lead to our favourite subject: boys.

'Well,' began Sam, lighting up a roll-up, 'I got talking to this boy while we were watching The Cure and . . . '

Beep. Beep. Beep.

'Oh bollocks — sorry, girls, gotta dash!' I said, untangling myself from the wooden pub bench. In the space of three minutes flat I'd run to the station as fast as my legs could manage after three halves of Strongbow. Ordinarily we would never drink on duty, but on an emergency shout no one questioned if you'd come straight from the pub — it was all hands to the pump.

As I turned the final corner I could see the usual Wacky Races-style scramble taking place as various retained firemen whizzed past in their cars while others ran towards the pump revving its engine on the forecourt. I had youth and agility on my side, however, and I dashed across the main road like an Olympic sprinter, ran through the open front bay door and, with a flourish, collected a tally and clambered onto the back seat. I'd made it!

'Where are we going?' I asked an equally out-of-breath Trevor as we set off at breakneck speed.

'An animal rescue, I think.'

'Oh, not another poor creature in distress,' I sighed, pulling my plastic leggings over my shorts, steel toecap wellies over my bare feet and a thick black wool jacket over my t-shirt. I hated thinking of animals suffering. I was fast learning that during the summer Thetford's acres of farmland acted as an adventure playground for all manner of livestock. I'd lost count of the number of cows we'd levered out of ditches and sheep that had been wedged upside down in drainage trenches, not to mention all the cats up trees and puppies stuck in drainpipes.

'OK, listen up, you lot,' said Nigel as we pulled up on a suburban side street. 'We've had a 999 call from Kilverstone Zoo. A South American monkey has decided that it's bored with living in captivity and has made a dash for freedom. From the sightings we've had from members of the public it's already crossed the A11 and the main London-Norwich railway line.'

He paused to mop his forehead with a pristine white handkerchief. It was ridiculously hot, but in the pump it felt more like a sauna with the thermostat turned to full. I felt a trickle of sweat run down my cheek. 'Our mission is to recapture this hairy beast and return it safely to the zoo,' he continued. 'The trouble is, these monkeys are as smart as hell, so it's not going to be that easy.'

Twenty minutes later, this was becoming all too obvious. 'The blinkin' thing could be anywhere,' said Trevor, echoing my own thoughts. We'd been ordered to spread out along the riverbank close to where the escapee had last been seen, 6 metres up a conifer tree. Greenfly skittered across the stagnant water, sending circular ripples towards where an abandoned bicycle was wedged in among the mud and the reeds.

'This is a bloody joke,' I said to Trevor, at the precise moment I noticed Nigel up ahead making an urgent chain-yanking motion to the pair of us. It was obvious what it meant: get your arses up here, now. Seconds later, we could see why. A furry, monkey-like shape was perched on the slate-tiled roof of the Nazarene Church on Crofton Road. 'She's been swinging from tree to tree ever since she made it across the A11,' explained a man in green overalls who, I quickly realized, was one of the zoo's keepers. 'The problem is, no matter how much fruit we tempt her with, she won't budge.'

To prove his point, he threw a banana towards the roof. The monkey watched it bounce off the tiles and roll into the gutter. Next, he threw a large bunch of grapes with the same result. We could be here some time. 'Maybe we should call her name?' I suggested. 'She hasn't got one,' he said morosely 'She's only just arrived with us. It's her second day at Kilverstone and she's already figured a way out by following her keeper's route off Monkey Island, which is completely surrounded by water. She's a smart one, all right.' I looked up again at the creature with renewed admiration. This was one strong female. The last thing I wanted was for any harm to come to her.

'OK, there's nothing else for it,' said Nigel, after the stalemate had carried on for a further half an hour. 'We're going to have to flush her down with the hose. Jo, you're the one with the feminine intuition, see if you can force her down on this side of the church so that she lands somewhere the keepers can grab her. And be careful. Judging by the looks of those teeth, she could bite your fingers off like a Kit Kat.'

It was a carefully choreographed operation: the shock of being doused with an icy blast of water sent our furry friend straight into the large net sprung by her relieved keepers. It had been a job well done, and by the time I'd dumped my firefighting gear and walked home it was 8 p.m.

It was still baking hot and I was ready to carry on drinking from where I'd left off with Kay and Sam, even if it was on my own. So when I let myself in, I was pleased to see Paul waiting for me with an open bottle of wine. Judging by the mischievous look in his eye, it wasn't the first one he'd consumed that evening. Paul had a perverse sense of humour, so I knew my hair-raising encounter would appeal to him. 'What, so the bionic Jo Reynolds is now single-handedly rescuing monkeys from church rooftops?' he said, kissing me on the neck. 'Is there nothing this woman can't do?'

Maybe it was the baking heat, the third glass of wine, or both, but I was disappointed when, having taken his t-shirt off, he jumped up from the sofa and darted into the bedroom. But I felt a tingle of excitement shoot through me when he reappeared holding the white belt from my judo outfit in his hands.

'I was thinking . . . how about we got up to some monkey business of our own?' he said suggestively, kissing me slowly on the lips. 'You're always so in control . . . perhaps it's time we turned the tables a little bit . . . '

He kissed me again. Christ, I hadn't been this hot and bothered since . . . let me think, breathing apparatus training. Hmm. Best not mention that now. 'You mean you want to tie me up?' I heard myself say huskily. Without saying a word, he led me towards the bedroom. Five minutes later, I was lying spread-eagled on the bed, completely naked. My hands were tied above my head using the judo belt and my feet were tightly bound to each bed post with a couple of silk scarves I'd handily remembered were in the little wicker basket on top of the chest of drawers. Cool air wafted through the open window as I writhed contentedly at the prospect of what was going to happen next. That is, until I heard Paul rummaging in the closet. What was going on? Instead of taking his clothes off, he was putting his shirt back on! 'Well, seeing as you're all tied up I thought I'd pop to the pub for a bit,' he said, grinning from ear to ear. 'I'll only be an hour . . . or two.'

And with that, he vanished, followed by the sound of footsteps and the front door closing behind him. Was he joking? A quarter of an hour later, I realized he wasn't.

'You bastard, Paul Clark, I'll get you for this!' I shouted out loud to myself, before bursting into a fit of giggles. I pulled at the ties. Not matter how hard I tried, I was unable to move. To compound my misery, I couldn't even reach my glass of wine.

Well, Jo, this is another fine mess you've got yourself into, I told myself, staring forlornly up at the ceiling. At which point, I heard an all too familiar sound coming from the crumpled pile of clothes on the floor. *Beep. Beep. Beep. Beep. Beep. Beep.*

Oh shit. It looked like I'd have to sit this one out.

15

(Don't Fear) The Reaper

The body was hanging 30 feet in the air.

We were deep in Thetford Forest, and suspended directly above our heads was the lifeless form of a twenty-five-year-old man. His body had been spotted first thing by someone walking their dog, and now it was our duty to get him down with as much dignity as we could.

'This ain't going to be easy,' said Nigel, taking a drag on his licorice roll-up. 'We can't put a ladder up there because the branch won't be strong enough to take the weight. We're going to have to cut him down.' We both looked up again. A strong gust of wind blew through the trees, causing the man's arms and legs to jiggle wildly like a rag doll. I felt myself shiver. This part of the forest, known as Emily's Wood, had always given me the creeps. Situated just east of Brandon on the Mundford Road, it had a gloomy, foreboding air that drew suicides like a moth to flame. The locals claimed it had been named after a seventeenth-century witch who made magic potions from the herbs and ferns found here, but whatever the reason, I was thinking I'd rather be anywhere else, when the low rumble of a car engine disturbed my thoughts.

While the police were already busy sealing off the area, Archie Solomon arrived. Rosy-cheeked and barrel-chested, Solomon looked more like a pub landlord than an undertaker, but his morbid sense of humour had made him a cult hero among my colleagues. As his low-slung black Citroën DS edged its way slowly towards us through the trees, we could hear loud music blaring through its open windows. Nigel looked round. 'Archie Solomon. He's like the Grim Reaper's right-hand man on earth . . . nothing fazes him.'

As the car got closer, I realized the loud music was in fact the theme tune from *The Munsters*. Was this guy for real? Nigel shot me a rueful grin, and I watched as Solomon levered his expansive bulk from the car and, beaming broadly, waddled over to where we were standing. 'Good morning, gentlemen — and lady,' he said, tipping the brim of his black felt fedora to me. 'What have you got for me on this fine morning?'

When Nigel pointed skywards, even Archie looked shocked.

'Oh, my,' he said, gazing up at the unhappy scene above our heads. 'That really isn't a good place to hang around, old boy.' As Solomon walked off, Nigel gave me a look, obviously aware of my rising anger. 'Don't take any notice of him, Jo. That's just Archie being Archie. You'll get used to him.'

I found it hard to watch as Ronnie climbed a ladder up to the man and carefully cut him down. It was awful. What must that man have been going through to end his life in such a way?

On the way back to the station in the pump I gazed disconsolately out of the window. Usually just driving through the Norfolk countryside was enough to lift my spirits, reminding me that, fundamentally, the world was a beautiful place. But not today. The more I stared, the lonelier and more depressing it seemed. Of all the things we had to deal with, suicides were the worst. It seemed ironic that we spent so much of our lives trying our best to rescue folk from accidents, fires and a hundred other everyday catastrophes. Yet when someone took their own life, we were as helpless as everyone else.

Most of the suicides that I'd seen so far were men. They all tended to follow a set pattern. They'd drive their cars deep into the forest, usually late at night. Once they'd found a quiet spot, they'd thread a garden hose from the exhaust pipe back through the driver's seat window. Most of the time they'd get back in, turn on the radio and let the carbon monoxide fumes do the rest. Usually the police would be notified by a dog-walker who'd seen an abandoned car. It was then our job to break into it and find the grisly contents. Even this apparently simple task was fraught with complications.

There was always a possibility that the person committing suicide had wired up the car so that it might explode, and we'd sit for hours deep in the forest, waiting for the bomb squad to turn up and pronounce the vehicle safe. In a job where tragedy was never far away, each one of these incidents cut me to the quick.

As the pump made its way back to the station, passing along the narrow, bumpy forest tracks and returning to the main road, it was a relief to leave Emily's Wood behind. In ten minutes we were in the slow-moving town traffic once more. I looked out at the people going about their daily business, scrutinizing each one in the hope they might give me a sign that everything was going to be all right. Most times, the sight of the fire engine would elicit the odd wave, usually from young boys out with their mums, but no one looked in my direction, or even smiled. My mind wandered back to the scene we'd just left in the woods. Was I *really* cut out for dealing with this sort of stuff for the rest of my career?

I desperately wanted some company. Rather than going home, I decided to go and see Chris. I'd finally split up with Paul after an almighty bust-up one Sunday evening when he'd refused to stay over. His refusal to commit to me full-time had driven me mad and it seemed pointless carrying on. The split seemed to push me towards Chris. After a few more Saturday afternoons renovating his house, we'd started going to auctions together in his battered Ford Cortina Mk3. This had then escalated into a series of clandestine meetings at his place where we'd dance around the living room to Fleetwood Mac's 'Go Your Own Way', the line 'Loving you isn't the right thing to do' ringing in our ears as we made our way upstairs to his Tudor four-poster bed. Moments of passion-killing hilarity would then ensue, as our bleepers would go off simultaneously at exactly the wrong moment. 'Hold that thought!' I'd yell as we both leapt out of bed, hoping we hadn't put each other's t-shirts or trousers on by mistake. I'd then cycle at full pelt to the station, knickers dangling out of the bottom of my jeans as Chris ran past me, making it look like we'd arrived from different directions, to keep our secret safe. He already had a girlfriend, and it played on my mind constantly, but I was nineteen and falling in love — nothing else seemed to matter.

★　★　★

Chris and I arranged that I could see him on Monday and Wednesday evenings and I quickly cycled back into town, looking at his shop from across the street to see if a particular upstairs light was on, which was my signal that it was safe to come round.

As I approached the shop, I could see it was still as cluttered as ever. A rusty suit of armour was in the window, one arm propped up against a Victorian rocking horse, with fairy lights draped over piles of antiquarian books, dusty oil paintings and pharmaceutical bottles made from brightly coloured glass. I smiled to myself. It really was one step up from a junk shop. When I pushed open the heavy wooden front door, I could see Chris standing at the far end, crouched over a table doing what appeared to be some detailed restoration work.

'I thought it might be you,' he said, not even looking up. He was delicately polishing one of his precious netsuke and was, as usual, deep in thought. 'I heard about what happened today,' he said. 'I guess you must be feeling pretty low. Well, the good news, Firefighter Reynolds, is that I have the perfect cure. Here, grab these!' In one quick movement he reached beneath the table and threw me one of his navy blue fire service t-shirts, a pair of boy's football shorts and a pair of old sneakers. 'Come on, let's go for a quick run,' he said. 'It'll do you good, I promise. There's nothing better for clearing the head after a long day.'

I was too tired to argue. And tonight's Miss Universe Sportswear Prize goes to me! I thought, as I reluctantly changed and followed him back out of the door.

It felt good to be out in the warm night air, and within minutes we were both running as fast as we could through town. I was always surprised at how quickly running made me feel better. As we sprinted along the towpath that snaked along the edge of the canal we were soon laughing and joking, switching to a gentle jog as we crossed the A11 at the traffic lights, and moved up along the sweeping roads to Abbey Farm. It was quiet now, and we picked up speed past the railway station and made our way along Station Road with its handsome Victorian villas and their postage-stamp front gardens all in a row. When we passed the little sweet shop, it was time for a final sprint, and we ran the last quarter of a mile back to his shop as fast as we could.

We'd timed it perfectly. By the time we'd had a shower and poured a large glass of Black Tower white wine each, it was time to lie in bed and watch our favourite TV show, *Hill Street Blues*.

As I lay with my head on Chris's chest, listening to the show's evocative theme tune, I felt myself start to relax.

'I didn't want to talk about it earlier, but what did you make of that terrible accident yesterday?' said Chris, just as I was settling down to enjoy the latest instalment in the life of the Hill Street police department. I knew what he was going to say, but I really didn't want to talk about it. *Not now*. I'd been pushing it to the back of my mind all day. But it was too late to stop him.

'I can't believe it myself — David Barton, dead.' David was the lovely, kind-hearted policeman who had let us into the fancy dress party when I'd stupidly turned up as an elephant. He'd been on duty when a lorry full of processed peas overturned on the A11 roundabout and he'd been killed instantly. Lovely David — who always had a smile and a friendly word for me when I saw him at RTAs during my first few months at Thetford — gone.

I tried to lose myself in the antics of my favourite characters, Captain Frank Furillo and his lawyer girlfriend Joyce Davenport, but it was impossible. Instead, my mind ran riot as a succession of grisly images flickered in front of my eyes.

First, poor David, then the awful suicide today. I knew these things were supposed to come in threes. I said a silent prayer. Was there something even worse still to come?

16

Bad Moon Rising

'I could kill you with one finger,' said a voice I didn't recognize. It was coming from the mess room. 'It's a little trick I picked-up in the Legion,' I heard the voice say. The Legion? Did he mean the British Legion? I put my ear to the door. 'You put your thumb up against their windpipe like this. Then one quick move and — snap.' The voice dropped into a sleazy Spanish drawl. '*Comer mierda y morir.*'

As I walked in, I could see that a crowd had formed around a stocky guy in his late twenties. He was sitting on a hard-backed chair from the canteen, which he'd turned around so that his muscular forearms were resting across the back of it, his legs spread wide apart. *Tough guy.*

'Oh, hello Jo, I didn't see you there,' said Nigel, as the crowd broke apart like a Terry's Chocolate Orange to reveal a man with the physique of a prize fighter — thick neck, chest like a drum, arms like cable. 'Meet the latest addition to our staff at Thetford . . . this

208

is David Blakeney.'

The man looked up. He had a shaven head, ears that stuck out like Toby jugs and two black beads where his eyes should have been. A pair of silver dog-tags nestled amid a rug of fuzzy black chest hair. Everything about him screamed 'trouble'.

'A pleasure to meet you, Miss Reynolds,' he said, rising to his feet. 'I've heard a lot about you.' As my hand disappeared into his, I felt it being crushed by a vice-like grip. I made a superhuman effort not to wince, knowing those beady eyes were looking for any kind of weakness. 'Pleased to meet you, too,' I said, catching a whiff of something. What was it? Oh yes. Brandy.

As if I'd been dismissed, he sat back down and pulled out a pack of cards. 'Right then, lads,' he said shuffling the deck with one hand. 'Who fancies a game of 'Chase the Ace'?'

⋆ ⋆ ⋆

As the weeks passed, it became clear that Blakeney was every bit as formidable as he looked. Like an Action Man brought to life, there didn't seem to be anything he couldn't do faster, quicker and better than anyone else.

'We don't need half this effin' equipment,' he growled one afternoon in the mess room, casting his eyes up at the 12-metre-high Training Tower. 'I could abseil down that using just a piece of rope, some webbing and an ordinary shackle off the pump.' Five minutes later, he was doing precisely that. You had to hand it to the guy — he could back up everything he said. His tales of fighting and whoring while in the French Foreign Legion, meanwhile, had transformed the mess room from a quiet place to enjoy a cup of tea into a macho clubhouse. 'Take my advice, lads, and stick to tarts,' I heard him say one afternoon as I munched on a custard cream. 'They're a lot cheaper and infinitely more effective.'

I also had a nagging feeling that I'd seen him somewhere before. I was changing into a clean t-shirt in the locker room after a hot, sweaty morning on the drill yard when he walked in unannounced. Normally, no one took any notice of me as I undressed, but I could feel his eyes boring into me from behind as I stripped down to my sports bra and pants. 'You don't remember me, do you?' he said, grinning lasciviously. I shook my head. 'Well, let me enlighten you. The first time I clapped eyes on you, you were eating a banana.' *Of course.* It had been on one of our early trips to Whitegates. I'd been in the mess room with the other boys having lunch when I'd noticed a man staring at me from across the room. That alone was enough to make me blush, but he'd also been moving his tongue in and out of his cheek to mimic someone giving a blow job.

'Oh, so you're that arsehole,' I said, slamming my locker shut and facing him. He stared back at me, his gaze drawn to my exposed right shoulder. He'd seen the small tattoo of a pair of cherries I'd had done on my arrival in Thetford.

'Only prostitutes have tattoos,' he said blankly. 'In fact, that's what I'll call you from now on — Fire Tart.'

Was this his idea of a joke? 'Listen,' I said, pulling on a t-shirt. 'It might be OK to behave like a moron in the Foreign Legion, but this is 1986. Women have rights. Or didn't that memo reach whatever cave you crawled out of? I've never been bossed around by any man, and I'm certainly not going to start with a sexist idiot like you.'

I was still fuming later that afternoon. We'd just come back from attending a shout on Burrell Way, on the outskirts of Thetford. There had been a fire in the degreasing tank of a plastics factory, and I'd led the BA crew that had located the source of the fire and put it out. It had been a tricky job, and the last

211

thing I needed was another run-in with Blakeney. As I was unlocking my bicycle to head home, I spotted him walking towards me. 'Hey, there's something I want to say to you,' he said, stopping in front of me. 'I know you haven't exactly taken a shine to me, and I'd like to make it up to you. I'd rather not talk about it here. Come and have a cup of tea with me after work.'

He had to be kidding. I'd rather stick needles in my eyes. 'No, thanks,' I said. 'Tempting as it sounds, I think I'll pass on that offer.'

'Seriously. I have something I want to talk to you about. Come on.' I considered for a moment. It was a flimsy premise, but what did I have to lose? Judging from what I'd seen of him already, if I said no, he'd only keep on bugging me.

'OK then. But just a quick cup of tea and then I'm leaving.'

'Great. See you at mine at seven.'

As I cycled home, I cursed my own stupidity. Why had I agreed to go?

* * *

My life was finally getting into some sort of order. I'd moved out of Ford Street and into a house closer to work on Melford Common. A mid-terrace flint cottage with a white front door, a sitting room with a fireplace and two decent sized bedrooms upstairs, it was, as my colleagues reminded me, another step up the housing ladder (trust them to think about ladders!). It also meant I was mortgaged up to the eyeballs, and to afford it, I'd taken in a lodger. Andy Bates had been on the same training course as me at Wymondham, and had just qualified. He'd been billeted to Thetford and had soon become like a second little brother to me. Better still, he also had a car, meaning that, as his landlady, I could always cadge a lift to the station.

Ordinarily, the two of us would have been spending a lovely quiet night in chatting away as we watched a repeat of *Shoestring*. Instead I was about to waste an evening in the company of a male chauvinist pig. Nonetheless, an hour later I'd showered, changed into my favourite outfit of jeans, t-shirt and green combat jacket and was standing outside Blakeney's house. I was, I realized, curious about what he wanted to tell me. The second he opened his front door, however, I knew I'd made a terrible mistake. He was wearing brown polished brogues, green corduroy trousers, tight around the bum, and a tight white t-shirt with the slogan 'Peace Through Superior Firepower'. 'Hello, Tart, I'm glad you could make it,' he said, beckoning me in.

213

'Welcome to my humble abode.'

'Good evening, David. And before we carry on can I make one thing perfectly clear. My name is Jo — not Tart.' He led me into a cramped kitchen. On the worktop sat a giant bottle of olive oil, six bottles of Spanish Fundador brandy, three bottles of gin and five pigeons. They were all still fully feathered and looked as if they were peacefully asleep. It was only when I poked one with my finger and its beady eyes looked back at me expressionlessly that I realized it was stone cold dead.

As he rummaged in the fridge, I shifted my gaze, looking for clues about his personality. I soon wished I hadn't. The walls were lined with bayonets, each one in its own metal holder. Had I stumbled into the home of a serial killer? It was becoming blindingly obvious that David wasn't the kind of man you sat around sipping tea with. Instead, he told me the drink choices boiled down to gin, or gin. What the hell? Now I was here it seemed pointless to argue.

After a couple of ridiculously strong gin and tonics, I started to relax. If this guy really was a serial killer, he would probably have got it over with by now, I reasoned to myself. And there was something quite endearing about how eager to please he was, despite the limited drinks menu.

'This is a recipe I learned in the Legion,' he said, placing a heavy pan on the stove. He added a large glug of olive oil and crushed four full heads of garlic on a piece of newspaper, roughly cleaning off the worst of the skin before dropping them into the hot oil. Watching him do this, my position softened. OK, so he was no Keith Floyd but there was a showmanship about his cooking that appealed to me. Maybe he wasn't quite as awful as I first thought. 'So what's with the t-shirt, Rambo?' I said, as he unfolded an old newspaper on the kitchen table and placed the dead birds on it.

'It reflects my outlook on life,' he said, taking a sharp knife and slicing through each of the pigeons' breast feathers. 'The way I see it, there are two types of people in this world — the hunters and the hunted.' He shot me a grin. 'Us hunters have to stick together.'

As the pigeons were cooking he told me a little bit about himself. It wasn't the 'hard knocks' story I'd imagined. He'd grown up in Norwich where his father had owned a furniture shop. His mother, I was amazed to learn, was a successful author who wrote romantic novels for Mills & Boon. He'd spent five years in the Foreign Legion and, up until arriving at Thetford, had spent the winters in

Spain and the summers in Guernsey. By the sounds if it, he was the archetypal rolling stone.

'You almost sound human when you talk normally,' I said, by way of response.

He skewered a pigeon breast on the tip of his hunting knife and offered it me.

'No thanks.'

'Come on, try it, Tart!' he said.

I was determined to show this he-man I could match him. And it did smell rather good. 'Listen, I'm not sure what's up with your hearing, but I'll eat it if you *stop* calling me Tart.'

★   ★   ★

Ten minutes and two more very large gins later, we'd scoffed the lot, straight from the pan. It was then he invited me up to his bedroom. 'It's OK,' he said, wiping a greasy hand across his lips. 'I won't make a pass at you.' I had to laugh. 'Come on, you've got to see it. I've painted it black.'

It really did seem pointless arguing. I was staggering up the stairs — bloody hell, those gins were strong — when the phone rang. Whatever strange spell he'd cast on me was instantly broken. His mood changed completely as he furtively cupped his hand over the mouthpiece in an effort not to let me hear. It was comical. 'Yes, darling. No, darling,' I overheard him say, meek as a mouse. 'No, I hadn't forgotten. No, I won't be late. I'll be there in ten minutes.' Clearly, the indomitable Mr Blakeney wasn't quite so tough after all.

As he poured another large gin 'for the road' it dawned on me I'd been there two hours and he still hadn't told me why he wanted to see me. 'So what did you want to talk to me about, David?' I said, knocking back the drink.

For a second, I could have sworn he looked bashful. 'Err, it's just that seeing you in action today in the degreasing tank made me realize I owe you an apology. I'm not used to working with a woman, and you're not like any woman I've ever met.' He raised his glass. 'I would be honoured if we could be friends.'

I weighed up how to respond. For a macho man like him, such an apology couldn't have been easy. 'Of course we can be friends,' I said, as we chinked glasses. 'Now get going. You don't want to be late for your date.'

As I walked home unsteadily, I couldn't wipe the smile off my face. My initiation into the strange world of David Blakeney had begun.

17

Burning Up Time

Beep Beep Beep. Beep Beep Beep.

It was August 1986, and it had been another stifling hot day at work. I'd just got in the door and was chatting to Andy, swigging apple juice from my favourite 'When God Created Man She Was Only Joking' mug, when our bleepers went off in unison. I hurtled up the stairs, grabbing any clothes that didn't look like they needed fumigating. By the time I got back down again, Andy was impatiently revving the engine of his beloved green Capri. He loved being behind the wheel, and I knew he'd get us there in record time. 'I'll drop you off as we arrive, don't wait for me, just get the pump,' he said as, exactly four minutes later, we screeched to a halt at the station's back entrance.

I lurched out of the car, grabbed a crew tally and my kit from the locker room and dashed through to the back of the pump bay. *Shit!* I'd missed it. The first engine was pulling away, its blue light flashing. However, I could see that the second pump was already revving its engine — both pumps were going!

Before anyone else could beat me to it, I leapt into the last remaining position on the back row and pulled the door closed firmly behind me. I was instantly glad I'd made it. Ronnie was in his usual corner position, and, judging by the smell of licorice, Nigel was in his customary position next to the driver.

'OK, listen up,' he said as we got under way. 'This could be a nasty one. There's a fire at Fogarty's. So get your kit on fast. If we need BA, I want you two — Jo and Ronnie — to go in there. But let's get there first and make an assessment.'

'Yes, Sub!' we both shouted back.

I looked over to see Ronnie winking at me. He was as thrilled as I was to be on a job like this. I knew from our familiarization visits that the Fogarty factory was the last building in Thetford anyone wanted to catch fire. A timber-framed building dating to the 1870s, it was being used as a treatment plant for bird feathers before they were transported to Boston in Lincolnshire to make pillows, duvets and mattresses. Timber beams, feathers, bedding — in firefighting terms, it all added up to the perfect storm.

We'd followed the trail of smoke through town, and as we turned left off the A11 into Minstergate, the scene in front of us took my breath away. The entire factory was on fire, and burning like the devil. The main two-storey building was being ripped apart from the inside, angry orange flames sending giant sparks and cinders shooting in all directions.

As well as our other pump from Thetford, there were at least five more crews on their way to the scene, but until they arrived it was down to us to do what we could. The sheer magnitude of the fire — the heat, the noise, the smell of burning wood — was jaw-dropping. I'd never seen anything like it.

'It's a bloody inferno!' said Ronnie, gazing up in awe as the 9-metre flames twisted and writhed against the night sky.

On Nigel's instruction we went into a well-rehearsed manoeuvre, four of us slipping the ladder from the back of the pump and under-running it to the base of the building before positioning it against an unaffected part. Once this was done we ran out the hose from the main pump, towards the foot of the ladder, attached the branch, and passed this to the two firemen who would be trying to control the blaze from this vantage point.

On a shout of 'Water on!' an icy jet of water hit the building, deliberately angled over the top of the gutter line to have maximum effect.

Our fight back against this huge blaze had begun.

I went to work, helping the guys to carry a light portable pump down to the nearby River Ouse and attaching a suction hose so that we had an almost limitless source of water.

While we were doing this, other crews arrived and I could see Nigel discussing the best plan of attack with his opposite numbers. A fire on this scale demanded a senior figure to take control. Assistant Divisional Officer David Mason, who was based forty-five minutes away in King's Lynn, was en route, as well as a mobile control unit.

In the meantime, some quick decisions needed to be made. I knew from all those months with my head buried in our red training manuals that this fire would take some stopping. Holes were forming in the old tiled roof, sucking smoke up into the sky and giving the blaze oxygen and fresh momentum. Added to this, the supporting walls would soon become unstable as the internal beams collapsed, making firefighting from within the building extremely dangerous.

There were also other considerations. With both of the station's pumps engaged in a potentially long and complicated incident, we had left Thetford without any cover. The golden rule of firefighting was that the town could never be left exposed. This meant that, like a giant game of chess, pumps from outlying stations would have to cover Thetford — and the other stations involved — until we all declared ourselves free and ready for the next job.

We'd been fighting the blaze for half an hour with little sign of progress when Nigel called us over to the furthest side of the fire ground. The scalding heat and choking, smoke-filled air made normal communication impossible. 'As you can see, we're in a pretty extreme situation right now,' he shouted, his face silhouetted by the flames. 'The feathers inside the factory are burning fast, and the fire is getting stronger with every minute that passes. There's a risk of the entire structure collapsing unless we move quickly. We need to access the inside of the building and fight the fire from within.'

He looked over to where I was standing. 'Jo and Ronnie, I want you to go in there and contain the fire. It's going to be tough, but we can't let it spread any further. Get your BA gear on, stand ready and wait for me to give the word.' As Ronnie and I rigged up our BA sets, heaving the heavy oxygen cylinders onto our backs and fastening the straps, my gaze was drawn to the fire in front of me. The flames were soaring above the rooftops, and the timber frame was disintegrating in front of our eyes — it looked like it could collapse at any second. Grim-faced fire crews rushed back and forth, dragging hoses through greasy black pools of water like slithering serpents.

I could almost feel my eyes dilating, and my heart was pounding so loudly it was making my temples throb. Stay calm, Jo, I said to myself, as we waited to hear when we'd be going in. Ten agonizing minutes later, Nigel walked back over to us. 'OK, you two, listen up. It's as I thought. We can't put this fire out from the outside. ADO Mason wants a crew inside and has found a good entry point. Remember, this is a two-storey factory with lots of heavy machinery. The middle floor is likely to be very unstable, so keep your wits about you. Get as far as you can into the building and do your best to put it out. We don't want any heroes, so take it slowly, and for God's sake, be careful.'

I gave him a silent thumbs up and handed in my tally at the control point where the BA board had been set up. It was my job to 'front' the hose with Ronnie behind me as second man. Big, strong and reliable, there was no one else I'd rather have watching my back. At the same time, it was my responsibility to keep both of us safe. I was the one leading us into danger — and one wrong move could be fatal for both of us.

I crouched low at the entry point. A side entrance on the far side of the building was still relatively unscathed, a few wisps of smoke the only clue to the blaze within. This was it. With the hose gripped firmly in the crook of my right arm, my BA mask in place and the full weight of the oxygen cylinder strapped to my back, I took a deep breath and stepped inside.

* * *

I'd walked into the filthiest, dirtiest oven on earth. Pitch black and as hot as hell, it knocked my senses for six. I edged slowly forwards, sweeping my right foot in an arc in front of me then shuffling forward with my left. The last thing we needed was for me to trip over any obstacles or stumble through some unseen gaping hole in the floor. As my eyes slowly became acclimatized, I could see that the thick roof timbers were burning away. The entire roof of the main workshop area was on fire from the inside, with fresh, smaller fires starting up each time a burning beam crashed down to the wooden floor or on the hundreds of boxes of feathers being prepared for treatment.

I adjusted the hose branch so that the jet was on a fine spray setting. I knew we had to be careful. The high walls on each side were beginning to lean in, and the power of the water jet on full power could easily trigger a collapse, sending the whole lot down on top of us. The noise was deafening, so with a low sweeping movement, I gestured to Ronnie that I was going to start spraying, and set to work.

A huge cloud of steam shot up as the fire hissed back at me furiously. I'd always seen fighting fires as mortal combat, and this one was the most vicious I'd ever faced. It would eat anything in its path to stay alive — including me.

We only had half an hour's worth of oxygen in our cylinders and I knew the only hope was to try to outwit it. I moved the jet around, spraying where I could have the most effect and picking off small pockets of fire before they could take hold. As we worked, I suddenly realized how exposed I was. My protective gloves were really nothing more than the thick plastic kind used for gardening, and the unprotected skin around my ears, neck and throat had started to prickle. I felt as if I was being cooked from the inside. At the same time, I knew I had a job to do and was determined to do it.

'There's no rush, let's do what we can and take it slow,' I shouted to Ronnie, echoing Nigel's instructions. I took another deep gulp of oxygen and remembered Paul and Eddie's mantra from our training: 'Urgent situations require cool heads'. There was no way I was going to let this fire beat me.

Visibility was now at zero, and I was concentrating hard when I felt a sharp tug on my right arm, pulling me backwards. Suddenly, a heavy wooden beam crashed to the floor right next to me. Somehow, in the swirling black fog, Ronnie had seen it falling and managed to grab me in time. We pressed on. With each step forwards, the discordant symphony of bangs, crashes and thuds grew steadily louder. I pictured cables pinging like violin strings, each distant rumble the sound of far-off drums. How could one building make so much noise?

As we ventured deeper into the interior I could see that the ancient timber beams were starting to buckle and break in the face of the fire's relentless assault. It was as if the air was being sucked out of the building, the little glass panes in the Victorian windows popping and shattering one by one. We had got as far in as we possibly could. Now we had to get out, and fast.

I thanked God for our guideline as we

threaded our way back out through the fumes and thick, toxic smoke, extinguishing pockets of fire as we went. As we emerged, I experienced a different, reverse kind of shock. It felt like I'd walked onto a film set. The evening had started to draw in, and massive artificial lights had been set up to light the building and help with the ongoing operation. I pulled off my face mask and helmet. Fresh air, at last! As I walked back across the fire ground with Ronnie, I saw Nigel walking towards us. 'Good work, you two,' he said once we'd handed in our tallies at the BA board next to the pump. 'This fire will take a while to put out, but we're slowly getting it under control. You did well in there, I know it wasn't easy.' He flashed us both a grin. 'Now go and have a fag break. You've earned it.'

★ ★ ★

'Got a light?' I said to Ronnie as the ashes from thousands of feathers blew in gusts around us. It always amused me that firefighters loved to smoke after a job, but I was as guilty as anyone. It just felt right, somehow.

The factory was now a blackened shell, with a large, but containable fire still raging within. It seemed impossible to think that anyone would be daft enough to go in there.

'You have to be bloody mad to do what we do,' said Ronnie, reading my thoughts, 'but I love every minute of it.'

I ran my fingers through my smoky, filth-encrusted hair. My eyes were streaming, I was soaked through with sweat, and every bone in my body ached. But I felt gloriously alive. 'You know what, Ronnie,' I said, blowing out a perfect smoke ring, 'I couldn't agree with you more.'

18

Addicted to Love

It was time to let my hair down. It was the Friday before Christmas, and I was thawing out in front of a log fire upstairs at The Central with Keith.

It had been a long week. I'd spent the afternoon at a plastics factory on Burrell Way. A young lad had trapped his arm in the hydraulic pressing plant, halting production of the company's bestselling Thomas the Tank Engine tea trays. It had been a hot, sweaty job cutting him free and by the time we'd managed it, the foreman had turned the air as blue as the poor lad's arm.

So much for the season of goodwill. Luckily, I'd bumped into Keith as I cycled home in the dark along Castle Street. If anyone could lift my spirits it was him. He'd lured me up to his den on the third floor with the promise of a smoke, a glass of champagne and a plate of homemade spaghetti bolognese. I hadn't taken much persuading. Cold wet slush was seeping through my socks, and I knew Andy was out at some Christmas drink-up. All that was waiting for me at home was a chicken and mushroom Fray Bentos pie and a packet of Smash.

Grace Jones's 'My Jamaican Guy' was on the stereo, Keith had rolled another perfectly constructed joint, and we were rummaging through the debris strewn across the coffee table for something to line the drawers of his latest acquisition — a 1950s cocktail cabinet he'd just bought from Chris's shop.

'You're turning into a hoarder,' I said, pulling a yellowing copy of the *Sun* from beneath a pile of old bills, discarded coffee cups and overflowing ashtrays. 'Not only is this place unhygienic, it's a bloody fire hazard.'

As I passed Keith the newspaper, he burst out laughing. 'It says here that Freddie Starr put someone's pet hamster in the microwave and then ate it between two slices of bread,' he said, passing me one of his expertly rolled joints. 'I can think of someone else who would do that.'

'Who?'

'Your new best friend Blakeney, of course. Or should I say, The Terminator.'

In the months since my peculiar evening with David Blakeney something odd had happened. We'd become good friends. I wasn't quite sure how it had happened, but I'd fallen into the habit of going out with Nigel, Chris and David after work. I was always keen to spend time with Chris, and these 'after work' drinks provided the perfect cover.

'I'll say one thing for him, he can knock them back,' he said, neatly folding the newspaper and placing it in the drawer of the glass cabinet. 'Takings are up massively since he started drinking here.' I could tell he was trying to be diplomatic, which, for Keith, wasn't easy. I passed him back the joint.

He took a leisurely drag, blowing the smoke out of the corner of his mouth. I loved the way he did that.

'Of course, at first I thought he was a total, top-of-the range, twenty-four-carat arsehole. Maybe underneath that hard man act there's an intelligent human being. Although the jury's still out, as far as I'm concerned.'

'Oh, he's not so bad once you get to know him,' I said, hearing myself sticking up for him. 'He's a useful bloke to have around the station. You just wouldn't want him to be the one calming you down if you were trapped in a car after an accident.'

This image sent Keith into a fit of giggles. 'What a thought. He'd probably try and rip the car apart with his bare hands.' After he'd recovered, he looked at me quizzically. 'He doesn't bother you, does he? He's always hitting on the barmaids downstairs. I'm sure he must have his eyes on you.'

The thought had genuinely never occurred to me. Go out with David Blakeney? He had to be joking.

★　★　★

It was a lipstick kind of night. New Year's Eve had rolled around again, and I was getting in the party mood at Melford Common with Kay, Sam and a large bottle of Smirnoff Red Label vodka. The last two hours had been spent in a cloud of hairspray and makeup while various dresses, scarves and jewellery had been scattered over my bedroom as we made vital decisions about what to wear. After much deliberation, we'd finally decided to get dolled up in matching short black dresses in tribute to our favourite video from *The Max Headroom Show* — Robert Palmer's 'Addicted to Love'.

'One, two, three — down in one, ladies!' shouted Kay as we each knocked back another shot. The cold liquid stung the back of my throat, and for a second I struggled to think straight. How many had we had? Six, I think. This was worrying. It was half past eight and I was already beginning to lose count.

'Listen, girls,' I said, sensing this situation would soon be sliding out of control. 'Let's make sure we've got everything we need before we go out, OK?' Kay and Sam nodded. I could tell from their eyes that they'd started drinking even before they'd turned up two hours ago.

'Three handbags?'

Check!

'Three coats?'

Check!

'Three packets of cigarettes?'

Check!'

I raised a shot glass.

'Come on then, down in one and let's go!'

★   ★   ★

Balloons, bunting, a bloody great banner reading 'Happy New Year 1987'. Whichever way you looked at it, The Central always threw a great party. The place was packed to the rafters. There was barely room to move, the pulsating throng seeming to move en masse as Bananarama's 'Venus' pumped from the speakers.

'Ah, home at last!' I said, breathing in the intoxicating smell of cigarette smoke, sweat, perfume and aftershave as we squeezed our way through the crowd.

I silently thanked God for my giraffe-like frame. I was practically six feet tall in my high heels, and could see David frantically signalling to us from the far side of the bar.

It was too busy to sit down, and I'd soon lost Sam and Kay in the ebb and flow of the crowd. I was contemplating a soul-destroying ten-minute wait at the bar for a drink when I spotted Chris. He was wearing a white shirt and jeans, both of which looked like they'd actually seen the inside of a washing machine. I'd never seen him looking so clean, fresh and, I had to admit, totally handsome.

'You're looking smart, are you expecting to see anyone?' I said, sidling over to him.

'Well, funny you should say that,' he said, craning his neck to look over the mass of bobbing heads. 'I'm actually looking for a certain firewoman who calls herself Jo. Do you know her?'

'I can't say I do.'

He looked me in the eyes. 'Funnily enough, someone told me that her twin had turned up wearing a little black dress. So if Jo can't make it, I guess her gorgeous twin will have to do.'

'Flattery will get you everywhere,' I said.

The opening bars of Berlin's 'Take My

Breath Away' started up. I loved that song. Without saying a word I kissed him full on the lips.

'Sorry to intrude on such a tender moment, darlings, but I've got a surprise for you both,' said Keith, grabbing my hand. 'Don't worry, it won't take a minute.'

Two minutes later we'd pushed our way through the crowds, passed through a pair of double swing doors and were standing in the hotel's spacious kitchen. Twelve magnums of champagne on ice were standing on a large wooden table next to fifty 1920s-style coupes. 'I haven't got enough for the whole bar, but frankly, most of them don't deserve it,' said Keith, grabbing a bottle and expertly removing the foil, muselet and cork in one smooth action. 'But I've saved one especially for the sole use of my two favourite firefighters. I'll leave you two lovebirds to it. I've got two hundred thirsty peasants to entertain.'

* * *

I looked at my watch. It was still only 11.15. We had forty-five minutes. 'Quick — follow me!' said Chris, grabbing the bottle and glasses as we slipped out of the side entrance.

Outside, the temperature had dropped to

235

near zero. It had been snowing on and off for days, and the grey slush on the pavement made walking quickly in my high heels practically impossible. A couple of freezing minutes later we reached the private passageway outside Chris's shop. 'Hurry up and open the door, I'm catching pneumonia out here,' I complained.

'I can't seem to find it,' he said, rummaging through a large set of keys.

'What do you mean, you can't find it?'

'I haven't got the key to the shop on me. It must be on my other set in my jacket pocket back at the pub.'

It was impossible to get angry with a man like this.

'What are we going to do with you, Mr Lancaster?' I said, draping my arms over his shoulders and leaning into him so that his back was pressed against the door. 'Something's got to keep me warm, so it looks like it's going to have to be you.'

'I'm taking a shine to you, Jo's twin sister,' he said, holding me close. I drew him towards me with my eyes, inclining my face towards his to make it obvious there was only one thing that could happen next.

For the next half an hour it was as though the space around us evaporated. There was just us, the doorway and the steadily emptying bottle of champagne. Nothing else mattered.

'Listen, I've been thinking,' he said, when we finally came up for air. Oh no. Please don't spoil it now. 'Why don't we go away somewhere together? I'd love to show you the Scottish Highlands. We could drive up there then come back down along the West Coast. There are palm trees up there, you've got to see it.'

Was I hearing him right? Had he just asked me to go away with him? I knew from our flying visits to their house on the other side of town that his mum and dad, Ada and Alan, were Scottish. My heart leapt. Maybe my luck in love was changing.

'I didn't know there were palm trees in Britain,' I said, as coolly as I could muster.

'Why don't you ask Nigel if you can take some holiday? When did you last take some proper time off?'

That was a good point. I hadn't taken a day off for months. I couldn't think what to say. I really didn't want to get hurt. But the thought of Chris, the open road, palm trees . . . 'Let me think about it.'

I looked at my watch. It was five minutes to midnight. It had begun to snow again, and I hugged him close, resting my head against his chest sleepily as large flakes, silver and dark, fell obliquely against the lamplight.

From across the street I could hear the music at the pub being cranked up. The Bangles' 'Walk Like an Egyptian' had just finished and the unmistakable throb of Prince's 'Kiss' had just begun. I was also, I suddenly realized, bone-chillingly cold.

'I'm going back to the bar,' I said, kissing him on the cheek. 'It's nearly midnight and I want to be with everyone for the countdown. If you're there later with your girlfriend, don't worry, I'll ignore you.'

I looked at his white shirt collar — it was covered in smudges of red lipstick.

'You'd better get cleaned up first, though.'

I stumbled back over the road into the warmth of The Central to find Kay and Sam. They hadn't even noticed I'd gone. The Pet Shop Boys' 'West End Girls' was blasting from the speakers, and a large tray of vodka shots was on the table.

'Here's to us!' said Kay, raising her glass, as an avalanche of streamers and brightly coloured balloons fell from the ceiling at midnight.

1987 would be a year to remember, I was sure of it.

19

Don't Leave Me This Way

'Seriously, is there anywhere on earth more beautiful than this?' I said, winding down the car window as the strains of Squeeze's 'Goodbye Girl' pumped from the stereo.

It was cold but dazzlingly bright, one of those days only the first week of January seems able to deliver. I stuck my head out of the window, closed my eyes and gulped down a lungful of the crisp, clean air.

'It tastes like . . . heaven.'

We were driving back to Thetford in Chris's Ford Cortina Mk3. We'd spent the day together in Diss and were on the forty-five-minute drive home. I could feel the magical world we'd lost ourselves in fading with each passing mile, and I was determined to savour every second.

We'd turned left out of town, heading west on the A1066. Shards of low winter sunlight had chased us as we'd weaved in and out of the woods, panoramic blue skies greeting us as we emerged out into the glorious, wide open landscapes of the Norfolk countryside.

I was wearing Chris's scarf and deerstalker hat, the heater on full blast as we sang along to Squeeze's *Cool for Cats* album, laughing and joking about the day's events.

It had been a productive trip. The day had been spent buying up items for his shop at the auction rooms on Roydon Road, and the car was jam-packed full of what a layman might call 'junk'.

On the back seat, we'd managed to cram in a vintage crystal chandelier, two cane-backed chairs, six Moorcroft pottery vases, a pair of Stone Age axe heads and a large box of stuffed birds.

'Who exactly is going to buy this stuff?' I said, looking over at Chris from my position in the passenger seat. He was back to his usual scruffy self, and was wearing jeans and an old green overcoat, a black Timex watch on his left wrist. I had to smile — he'd never be a Rolex kind of guy.

'What you have to understand, Jo, is that the antiques game is about putting your personal opinions to one side, and thinking about the resale value,' he said, the constant *thump-thump-thump* overhead reminding me that we'd also strapped a heavy wooden church pew to the roof rack, covered in a floral quilt. 'One man's rubbish is another man's priceless collectible.'

'If you say so, Lovejoy.'

* * *

I treasured these outings. We were still getting to know each other, but I loved having a life outside of the fire service. Away from prying eyes, Chris and I were free to be who we wanted to be. To the eclectic bunch at the auction house — crusty colonels, bookish academics, other dealers — we were just a loved-up couple looking for a bargain. It was only as we got closer to home that our true identities were revealed. I wasn't sure how our relationship would pan out, but being with him just felt right. We didn't talk about his girlfriend — we both knew things weren't right as they were, but I didn't want to force him to choose. All I cared about was the time we spent together.

As we approached the turning for Castle Street, the heavens opened. A light drizzle had built steadily into hard, driving rain. I looked dolefully out of the window. Each of the familiar landmarks — the Castle mound, the Albion pub — seemed to be mocking me, telling me that I was coming back down to earth with a bump.

By the time we pulled up outside his shop, the spell had been well and truly broken. I looked down the passageway: it already felt like a lifetime since New Year's Eve. Our trip to Scotland hadn't been mentioned all day. Even if it had, I wouldn't have known what to say.

While I was obviously tempted, I was worried about what the guys at work would think. I'd worked bloody hard to be accepted on equal terms. As a woman I'd constantly had to go the extra mile to prove that I could match the men. Would my position be compromised if they knew I was dating one of their colleagues? Would I suddenly be seen, first and foremost, as 'Chris's girlfriend' and a firefighter second? The thought appalled me. The station was a hive of gossip. If they didn't know about us already, they undoubtedly would by the time we got back.

I suddenly felt overcome with exhaustion. Normally I'd have done anything to prolong our time together, but it had been a long, tiring day. He unlocked the side alley door, walked in a few paces, and beckoned for me to follow. When he turned around, I shook my head. 'I'm going home, Chris. I'm tired. Thanks for a fun day.'

He smiled and nodded. He could always read situations like this. 'OK, Jo-Jo, thanks for all your help today — drinks are on me next time I see you.'

'Make it dinner and it's a deal.'

★ ★ ★

I was walking in a winter wonderland. It had been snowing steadily since New Year and the whole of Thetford was covered with an elegant white blanket.

The pretty flint cottages looked picture-postcard perfect, the market square with its handsome buildings like something from a TV adaptation of *A Christmas Carol*. It was the soundlessness I loved — it was as if someone had put mufflers on the world.

As usual, I'd worked on Christmas Day. This suited me perfectly. I'd never felt the urgent draw some people have to spend it with their parents, and it also meant the other guys could spend it with their wives and children.

There was very little going on, and I'd sat in the mess room with Ronnie and a couple of the others, watching TV and eating my body weight in cold turkey sandwiches and mince pies.

The world seemed to grind to a halt at this time of year, the only blips of excitement an occasional chimney fire or somebody's Christmas tree lights catching fire. Even then, you felt people only called 999 as a last resort. Who really wanted a load of burly firemen — and me — traipsing across their living room during the Queen's Speech?

* * *

It was a couple of days after our trip to Diss, and I'd agreed to meet up with Chris, David Blakeney and Andy Bates for a post-Christmas drink. The original plan had been to meet for lunch then go on a pub crawl, but this was soon abandoned — it was just too much fun at The Central.

I'd started off drinking red wine, and for some reason had progressed on to port. I couldn't get enough of the stuff — it tasted like alcoholic syrup. And it kicked like a mule. By mid-afternoon we were all at that tipping point between tipsy and sloshed, the hinterland between sense and nonsense. The boys had moved onto shorts — David on brandy, Andy and Chris on whisky — and were mucking about, feeding food from the kitchen to Keith's two Dobermans,who both had flashing red plastic antlers tied to their heads.

Eventually the dogs got bored, and talk moved, inevitably, to the subject of work. 'So, Firefighter Reynolds, what are your ambitions for 1987?' said Andy. He knew I'd passed my

Leading Fireman exams and was always teasing me about my future plans. 'I reckon you'll be running the show by the time you're thirty,' he said. 'I can just see you sitting in Chief Officer Hogg's chair at Whitegates, telling everyone what to do.'

His glazed expression told me he didn't want a serious response, and I wasn't about to give him one. 'Well, it's about time a woman was in charge,' I said jokingly. 'To quote The Stranglers: 'Liberation For Women — that's what I preach.''

I downed another glass of port. Wow. The stuff really was delicious. I pointed a finger at Andy, who appeared to have cloned himself. I was seeing double.

'You'd better pull your socks up, Andy Bates. Otherwise I'll post you somewhere out in the Fens, as far away from bars, women and motorbikes as I can make it!'

I made direct eye contact with Chris.

'And who knows,' I said, 'maybe this year I'll find time for a little holiday, too.'

Chris winked at me, and I took it as my cue to go over and sit on his lap. He was wearing a bright red jumper I hadn't seen before and I tugged at it playfully

'Is this a new Christmas jumper?'

'How did you guess? You know mums and their presents. I've got to be seen in it at least once, and you're lucky enough to have witnessed it.'

I put my arm around him. David and Andy knew about the two of us, and we were all in that convivial post-Christmas mood where nothing really matters, until closing time, at least. As I stood up, the room seemed to tilt sideways. *Whoa.* I was way more drunk than I thought. It really was time to leave.

'Au revoir, mes enfants!' I said, kissing them each goodbye as I made my way gingerly to the door. 'Don't do anything I wouldn't do.'

An arctic wind hit me as I came out of the cocoon-like warmth of the pub. The cold air made me feel even more drunk, and for a split second I didn't know where I was going, literally or figuratively. Should I go home, or maybe see what Kay and Sam were up to? They were sure to be up for a drink. A wave of tiredness hit me even thinking about it. It was time to go home.

I turned right and walked briskly back to Melford Common in the fading light, trying not to slip or slide on the lethal frozen pavements and roads. It was too cold to snow, and I pulled my scarf tight around my neck and lowered the flaps of my deerstalker to cover my ears.

Shit! I was still wearing Chris's stuff. I'd

forgotten to give them back from the other day. For a moment I thought about traipsing back to The Central. No, I couldn't face it. I'd give them back next time I saw him.

I pulled the hat low over my eyes and headed home. After a long soak in the bath, I'd changed into my pyjamas and towelling dressing gown and curled up on the sofa to watch TV. The combined effects of the wine, port and my little log fire had lulled me into a deeply relaxed state, and I must have fallen asleep. I woke up to an almighty banging at the door. A loud voice, too, shouting my name. As I gathered my wits I recognized the voice — it was David.

I unlocked the door and he stepped quickly inside, slamming it shut. He was soaking wet and dressed in full camouflage gear. There was something about him I couldn't put my finger on. He seemed . . . different.

'Get me a towel, I'm freezing.' His voice sounded odd. I ran into the bathroom, grabbed a towel and threw it to him. As he stood drying himself, I could see his hand was shaking. David Blakeney, shaking? What the hell was going on?

'For God's sake, what's wrong?' I grabbed his arm. 'You're scaring me.'

For the first time he looked me in the eye. 'We can't find Chris.'

'What do you mean, you can't find Chris?'

After they'd left the pub, the three of them had gone back to Chris's house to continue drinking. This had carried on for hours until Chris had decided he wanted to go out shooting ducks on the river. The others had tried to dissuade him, but he'd insisted. He'd already shot and plucked one when the second duck he'd shot had landed in the river. Chris had then dared the other two to jump in and retrieve it.

'The river had ice floating in it,' explained David. 'It was madness to even think about going in there.' He paused and shook his head. 'That was when Chris jumped in.'

I couldn't believe what I was hearing.

'After a couple of minutes he hadn't surfaced. We both dived in after him but the water was so cold we were in danger of passing out. We were wondering what to do when a police car pulled up. But instead of organizing a dive team they took us down to the station and interviewed us.'

He looked at his watch. 'I've just come from there, and there's still no sign of Chris.'

'So he's missing?'

'Yes, and someone really needs to go and tell his parents.'

I could feel my heart beginning to beat faster. One thing was blindingly obvious

— there was no way David could go. He looked awful. There was no other alternative. 'I'll go,' I said.

I raced upstairs, pulled on my Levis and a big black jumper and splashed some water on my face. As I ran towards the front door, I could hardly bear to look at David. He looked terrible, a shadow of the man I knew. 'Have a bath, and for God's sake don't drink anything but coffee.'

He nodded.

A wave of hysteria washed over me. I had to get it out of my system before I arrived at Chris's parents' house. I howled inside my head, screaming with anger and frustration. How could they have been so stupid?

My legs felt like lead as I forced myself to make the ten-minute journey across the common. Dawn was breaking, the warmth of the morning sun sending crazy notions into my head. I had a sudden urge to run — run as fast as I could in the opposite direction.

From the moment I knocked on the door, I felt like a character acting out my worst nightmare as a three-act play, each scene more horrible than the one before. First, his parents' ashen faces as I explained to them what had happened. Then, the anxious wait. Finally, the shadow of the police uniforms through the stained-glass front door. When the doorbell finally rang, we were drinking tea from bone-china cups, served on a bamboo tray.

As gently as she could, a policewoman explained that divers had just found Chris's body. I looked up at the clock on the mantelpiece. It was 10 a.m. precisely on 8 January 1987.

★ ★ ★

'You've got to be kidding,' I hissed. 'Not *him*. Not now. Not today, of all days.'

It was another bitterly cold day, and I was standing outside St Cuthbert's Church in Thetford with Nigel, David and Trevor Leggett. We had just attended Chris's memorial service, and, as pallbearers, were due to travel with the body to the crematorium in Norwich.

I'd been dreading this part of the day most of all, but it was only when I saw the roly-poly figure of Archie Solomon behind the wheel of the hearse, I realized he was going to drive us there. 'If he says something, I swear I'll kill him,' I said to Nigel under my breath as he pulled up. 'Stay strong, Jo,' he said, as the four of us shuffled along the black leather back seat. 'Don't rise to it. And whatever happens, don't cry.'

For the first few days after Chris's body had been found I'd felt completely numb. After the initial flood of tears, I'd retreated into my shell at Melford Common, unwilling and unable to take in what had happened.

I'd borrowed one of Chris's soft fawn jumpers one day and never got around to giving it back. He'd worn it to mine and Sam's joint twenty-first birthday party, and I had a photo of us taken that night where we'd both looked happy, relaxed and at one with the world. I started wearing it every day.

Cocooned in the white double quilt off my bed, I'd play Fleetwood Mac's *Rumours* over and over again. Christine McVeigh's 'Songbird' had always been 'our' song, but now the lyrics felt almost as if they'd been written for us, convincing me there was a new, very scruffy angel in heaven, looking out for me.

The accident was all anybody could talk about, but it seemed pointless to me going over what had happened. The outcome was always the same. Chris was dead, and nothing could bring him back. The coroner had taken a similar view at the inquest and recorded a verdict of 'death by misadventure'. I couldn't help but smile — Chris would have liked that.

A large crowd had gathered at the church, most of whom I didn't recognize. In the back of my mind I'd known that Chris had lots of friends, but I'd only ever really seen him alone or in the pub with David and the others.

A polished parquet floor ran the length of St Cuthbert's, separating rows of dark oak pews, each framed by white stone arches and decorated with brightly coloured prayer cushions. I scanned the packed pews for Nicky, his girlfriend. Compared to her, I realized I barely knew Chris, and could only imagine what she was going through now.

Christ, I hated funerals. I couldn't stand how public and formal they were. If it had been up to me, I would have taken his ashes into the forest and planted a tree in his memory. He was at his happiest when he was roaming around in the wilderness. It wasn't my call, though. Through the eyes of everyone present, I was just a work colleague.

No one had banked on such a big turnout, and we were squeezed in so tightly along the pew that I could barely move my elbows to open my hymn book. I let my mind wander, revisiting all the good times I'd had with

Chris rather than engaging with what was going on. There had been a real synergy between us. Even the most simple of activities — watching TV, going for a run, having a day out — became fun when it was with him. Even as a firefighter, the thought of how dull life was going to be without him terrified me.

I saw years and years of 'normal life' stretching out ahead of me. I was twenty-one, and my friends were already getting married and having children. The thought of a stable family life, and that kind of routine, scared me to death.

Chris was only thirty but he'd been to the four corners of the world. There wasn't anywhere he hadn't been, yet he treated his experiences like a walk in the park. Now that he'd gone it felt like I'd lost my teacher, my friend, my lover and my purpose.

The wheezing of the church organ and the shuffling of people getting to their feet shook me out of my trance-like state. I'd somehow managed to zone out for the whole service. Now the only hurdle left to negotiate was the one I'd been dreading the most — the trip to the crematorium. As we filed out of the church, I could see Archie Solomon sitting behind the wheel of the hearse. Christ almighty — was he revving the engine? My teeth were already on edge as I shuffled along the back seat, squeezed between Nigel and David with Andy by the far window.

The crunch of the wheels on gravel gave way to the velvet purr of the engine as we slowly turned into King Street. The light was fading fast, the sodium glare of the streetlights bathing the shopfronts in an eerie dark blue glow.

I had to remain focused on the task ahead. We still had to carry the coffin into the crematorium. If I let myself start thinking that his body was in the back of the car, I'd break down completely. Inhale, exhale, I told myself as I began to well up. I had to stay strong. If only there wasn't this crushing, all-pervasive silence . . .

At that exact moment I heard a voice pipe up from the front seat. It was Solomon.

'I say, it's deathly quiet back there,' he said. 'Anyone would think someone had died or something.'

I felt like jumping out of my seat, grabbing the guy by the throat and throttling him. I looked to my left. Nigel's face had gone a shade of purple. But he wasn't angry. *He was trying not to laugh.* I looked to my right — David and Andy were the same. What was wrong with them?

'Anyway,' continued Solomon, 'I'm glad

you're all here because I'm thinking of opening up my own antiques shop.'

I felt the others take a sharp intake of breath. My head was beginning to spin. Solomon paused, looked in the rearview mirror, and then raised his voice ten decibels. 'Hey Chris, could you give me any tips?' There was a moment's pause, like the gap between thunder and lightning. Then every single one of us burst into hysterical laughter.

It was as if a safety valve had finally been opened. For the next twenty minutes I laughed so much it hurt, tears running down my face as a tidal wave of conflicting emotions — love, anger, frustration, sadness, sorrow — poured out of us in a cathartic tidal wave of shared jokes, stories and high jinks.

I daren't think what other road users must have made of it as we trundled along the A11, but in those glorious, anarchic, unfettered and utterly un-PC minutes I finally, truly understood what it meant to be a firefighter. It was our way of saying goodbye. We weren't being cruel. It was the furthest thing from cruel. It was our way of acknowledging that the only way to deal with death was to laugh in its face and carry on regardless. After all, what was the alternative? Mope around? That was never going to happen with these guys.

I'd known firemen were special ever since that day I'd sat on the damp grass and watched Ben-y-Mar burn down when I was twelve. But as we sat there laughing ourselves senseless at the sheer bloody, beautiful mess we call life it became clearer than ever.

The outside world would never see things the way we did. But that was because they never *saw* the things we did. We didn't live by the rules, because the things we dealt with existed outside normal boundaries. I couldn't include myself, but I knew these men were the best we've got — the ones who would walk into a burning building to save a complete stranger. For twenty glorious minutes, we reminded each other of the special, unshakeable bond we shared.

'Thanks, Archie, I really needed that,' I said as we pulled up outside the crematorium, our faces now as solemn as the occasion demanded. 'I thought you might,' he said quietly. 'Think of it as part of the service. Now, go in there and do what you have to do, and get through this the best you can.' He gave me a wink, and leant in towards me so no one else could hear. 'And just be grateful I didn't play the *Munsters* theme when I turned up to meet you.'

As we lifted the coffin proudly onto our shoulders, no one else present at the crematorium was any the wiser about what had just happened. But a massive weight had been lifted. We were firefighters. Nothing could defeat us. Not even death.

20

Pull Up to the Bumper

I was back in the saddle. Rather than brood at home, Nigel had suggested I come into work to take my mind off what had happened. As always, it had been good advice. Not only was I back on duty, I was in the driver's seat of a 10-tonne Ford 'D' Series truck — commonly known as a fire engine.

It was the final day of my long awaited HGV 3 test. Unlike a normal driving examination, this spanned an entire week, and seemed designed to weed out those applicants with any kind of weakness.

I'd applied for the test nine months earlier, in the week I'd turned twenty-one. It had been my ambition to get behind the wheel from the minute I'd signed up at seventeen, and I knew there was a long waiting list even once I'd had my name put forward as a suitable candidate. So when Nigel had called me into the front office one day and told me I'd got my test date I was ecstatic.

I'd been given a thick *Roadcraft* manual to study and in the months since had spent any quiet period at work asking Trevor and Ronnie to quiz me on the highway code. Two large metal 'L' plates had been ceremonially wired to the front and back of one of the station's two pumps, and under Nigel's calming influence — with the rest of the crew ribbing me constantly from the back seat — I'd been out and about on the Norfolk back roads. It was totally different to driving a car. The huge black steering wheel was twice the size of a normal one, and compared to my old Avenger the dashboard looked like something from the Starship Enterprise.

I'd mastered reversing through hours of practice in the car park of the Jeyes factory on the outskirts of town, but the 400 gallon water tank situated in the belly of the vehicle made handling, especially around corners, a lot trickier. As designated driver I also had to be able to read the rev counter, compound gauge, pressure gauge and tank sight tube, all located in the pump bay.

As the test date approached, the mickey-taking from the rest of the crew had steadily increased. For some of the guys, especially Ronnie, driving the fire engine was a hassle he could do without. 'Think about it, Jo,' he said one day when my enthusiasm was clearly getting too much to bear, 'what, really, are the upsides of driving the pump? At best you'll be a hero when you get us to a shout in record time. But most of the time you'll have people shouting at you to get there faster or blaming you when we're seconds too late to save someone, when not even Niki Lauda could have got us there quicker. On top of all that, you don't get a single penny extra for it.'

I knew that deep down this was all harmless fun, and that all of the guys — *especially* Ronnie — had been secretly willing me on.

★ ★ ★

At the beginning of my HGV 3 training I'd been tested on vehicle manoeuvring, gear change exercises and general driving skills. On Tuesday, we'd driven into Norwich to see how I handled a city environment. Wednesday had been a long-distance drive to Cambridge along the M11, and the previous day I'd had an hour-long sit-down theory exam. Today was the day of my actual driving test, and things had, I thought, been going well. Without a moment's hesitation I'd steered the engine right out of the station forecourt, and for the last hour I'd taken us on a seamlessly executed guided tour of Norfolk.

As I'd carefully parked back on the station forecourt, Colin the examiner made a few final notes on his clipboard before folding his hands in his lap and looking directly at me. 'Thank you for a very interesting week, Firefighter Reynolds,' he said, looking at me evenly. 'I only had to close my eyes once.' I could feel the butterflies rising in my stomach. Did this mean I'd passed, or not? He broke into a smile. 'Accordingly, I'm pleased to tell you that you are now qualified to drive this appliance to HGV 3 level. I think that this may be a first for both of us. And as far as I'm aware, you're the only female firefighter qualified to do so. Well done.'

I concentrated so hard on freezing the moment in my memory for ever that my head ached.

⋆   ⋆   ⋆

Just under a month had passed since Chris's funeral and life was slowly getting back to normal. Aside from those few painful minutes every day when I had to assure Andy, Sam, Kay, my mum, Malcy, Keith, Mike and anyone else who asked that I was fine — *absolutely fine* — life had carried on pretty much as usual. Perhaps that was down to the nature of the job; there was never time to dwell on anything. Spring was in the air, the clocks had gone forward, the worst of the cold weather had passed, and it felt like time to stop moping around. I folded Chris's fawn jumper neatly and put it in the cupboard. From now on, I decided, it would only be worn in moments of acute emotional anxiety.

*   *   *

I'd become increasingly friendly with David Blakeney. I'd felt a bit lost since that tragic evening and I think our shared grief brought us together. We'd spend quiet evenings after work in The Black Horse, ending up at the Star of India restaurant on White Hart Street as we got to know each other better.

The more I learned about him the more fascinated I became. A born rebel, he'd joined the French Foreign Legion on leaving school, only to leave after completing the two-year training course. He'd then drifted between various odd jobs, but missed the old lifestyle so much that he'd walked into a police station in Madrid and asked to be taken to the nearest outpost of the Spanish Legion (whose motto, charmingly, was 'Long Live Death'). They'd accepted him as a non-Spanish national on two conditions: he gave up his passport and burned his clothes. The tales he told me made my hair stand on end. Life in the Legion made my experiences with ADO Gallagher look like a teddy bear's picnic. I liked his self-assurance. Nothing fazed him.

I'd asked him round for Sunday lunch and we were tucking into roast pork with crackling washed down with red wine when he asked me to go on a day trip to Cromer. It seemed like a good idea. I'd always loved the seaside, and it would be a chance to get some fresh air and forget about work for a couple of days.

We went the following Sunday. The sun was shining and we'd both booked ourselves absent from the fire station rota, giving the trip an illicit, 'bunking off school' aspect. David had borrowed a car for the day, and we headed east past Norwich on the ring road with Wham's 'Freedom' blasting from the CD player.

We were walking along the Victorian pier when he put his arm around me. The chilly sea breeze was going straight through my t-shirt and cotton jean jacket, but it wasn't just the warmth I appreciated. It was comforting to have him so close. We held hands as we walked back to the car through town, but the crackling sexual tension wasn't released until the drive home. We stopped at a red light on Colman Road, and suddenly we were kissing, our lips locked together in a passionate embrace for several minutes. Red light spells danger, I thought to myself, as the cars behind were forced to navigate their way around us, beeping their horns as they went.

Once we were back in Thetford I was plagued by the same old fears. I was worried about what everyone at the station would think, and to take my mind off it, I concentrated on my future prospects. I'd already passed my Leading Fireman exams, and now I'd done my HGV 3 test, I was already thinking about the next step up — promotion to sub officer.

★ ★ ★

I knew David was bored and fidgety at work, restless for more adventures, but it still came as a shock when he told me that he was leaving. 'I've been offered a job fixing generators on an expedition to Peru, Tart,' he informed me casually one night in The Black Horse. I'd grown used to him calling me 'Tart', and secretly quite liked it — it had become an affectionate nickname between us, and a reminder of our initial falling-out in the locker room.

'Well, that's a bolt from the blue,' I replied, feeling — I realized — like the floor was giving way beneath me. 'When do you leave?'

'Next month.'

As the weeks ticked by to his departure date, we became closer and closer. I've always been good at organizing other people's lives, and we planned the entire trip together, right down to me escorting him to London for his jabs and helping pick out his new wardrobe (which at least would mean the end of his hideous green cords!).

It all seemed wildly exotic, and I harboured crazy thoughts that one day I, too, would escape the daily grind as we booked his one-way flight from Heathrow to South America, with only a rucksack as luggage. David made it all seem so easy.

I cried as his National Express coach pulled out of Thetford, and I couldn't help but see it as a mirror image of those bus journeys with Malcy from Ben-y-Mar to see my dad in Norwich. This time, the colour was draining out of my life, with little or no prospect of it returning. Summer drifted into autumn, the weeks into months. The only bright spot would be an occasional scribbled postcard. I threw myself into work to forget about him, and lived for the moments when the red phone in the watch room would ring.

★　★　★

The danger had been reported by a member of the public. Five blue and white oil drums had been spotted on a forest track near Weeting, and we had been called out to investigate. The policeman first on the scene had reported that they were all labelled 'methylene chloride' and that one of them seemed to be leaking.

Once this news had reached the fire service, he had immediately been dispatched to the West Suffolk Hospital for a precautionary check-up. He had unwittingly stumbled upon some barrels of highly toxic chemicals, and a full-scale alert was now in progress.

The surrounding roads had been closed, the brigade's Chemical Incident Unit was on hand and ADO David Mason — based at King's Lynn — was in charge of figuring out what to do with the oil drums.

'If I was a betting man, I'd say that they've fallen off a lorry on their way to one of the factories on the edge of town,' explained Nigel once we'd arrived on the scene. 'This stuff is more commonly known as dichloromethane — they use it as a paint-stripper or a degreasing agent. Either way, it's dangerous stuff. The human body turns it into carbon monoxide. Breathe too much of it and it's Goodnight Vienna.' He paused and took a drag of his licorice roll-up. I had to hand it to him. No one paused quite like Nigel. 'At the very least, inhalation can leave you with nausea and a very nasty headache.'

After he'd consulted with David Mason over the best plan of attack, Nigel walked back over to where I was standing with Ronnie. 'OK, listen up, you two,' he said, his tone now all business. 'I need you to take a good look at these drums. If one of them *is* leaking, you'll have to try and seal it. The last thing we need is this stuff spilling everywhere. It's a hazard to wildlife as well as Joe Public. So look lively, I need you back here in five minutes wearing your breathing apparatus gear and full chemical protection suits.'

That was easier said than done. The protection suits were made of a thick, plastic-like material and went on *over* our basic firefighting kit, including our heavy black wool coats. On top of that, we had to strap on our oxygen cylinders and attach our face masks. By the time I'd got everything on, I could only move at a snail's pace, which was probably for the best — a job like this wasn't to be rushed.

A 15-metre exclusion area had been set up by the police, preventing anyone from entering the strip of grass next to the road where the drums had been abandoned. The closer we got to them, I began to see why. It was obvious one of them *was* leaking, a clear liquid oozing into large puddles on the forest floor.

★ ★ ★

It was now our responsibility to sort out this situation, and I could feel my adrenalin levels shoot up. The weight of our equipment meant we were both already breathing hard through our mouthpieces, and the task of moving the drums, each of which held 45 gallons of liquid, wasn't going to be easy. We would need all our strength, awareness and focus to do it.

'OK, Jo,' said Ronnie to me through the headset, gesturing to an empty drum slightly away from the others. 'Let's drop the empty drum over the leaking one like a sleeve. On a count of three — lift!'

I gripped the empty drum as tightly as I could through my protective gloves as we heaved it into place. A sound similar to fingernails being raked down a blackboard followed as metal scraped against metal. A quarter of an hour later we were still trying, but to no avail. It wasn't going to work.

We had been so engrossed in these attempts that the emergency whistles on our suits had started to sound, meaning we were down to our last fifteen minutes of air supply. 'Time for Plan B, I think, Jo,' said Ronnie, signalling to me that the only option left to us was to seal the leaking drum the best we could using thick polythene sheets.

Our air cylinders were practically empty by the time we'd managed it, and I could tell from the rest of the crews' frantic signalling from the other side of the cordon that it was time for us to call it a day.

'Good work, you two,' said Nigel as we both collapsed on the grass verge, totally spent. Before we could change out of our suits they needed to be decontaminated using high-pressure jets. This process shouldn't have been fun, but somehow it always was, a tacit acknowledgement of a job well done.

'You two look like you've just run the Grand National!' said Trevor as we eventually peeled off the suits, releasing enough steam to fill a sauna.

The punchline came the next day. Nigel walked into the mess room to tell us that laboratory tests on the drum we'd sealed had proved it contained nothing more deadly than H_2O. It turned out that one of the local factories had cleaned and reused the drums, without thinking to remove the labels. We'd been through all that for nothing.

I looked over at Trevor, who by now had a huge grin on his face. 'Don't say anything,' I said, as he collapsed into a heap of laughter.

* * *

With David gone, my social life had ground to a complete halt. One night, Andy and I were sitting in my kitchen, testing each other on bizarre facts from *The Guinness Book of World Records* ('So Andy, can you tell me exactly how much the fattest dog in the world weighs?'), when the phone rang.

We looked at each other. Since Chris's death we'd both been acting like hermits, and no one ever rang after 9 p.m. The voice at the end of the line sounded like it was coming from Mars. But it was unmistakably David. My heart lurched. He'd been gone for three months, and it scared me how much I'd missed him. He explained that he was still in deepest, darkest Peru and was ringing from a ramshackle post office.

'I've had a bit of a time of it,' he said, his voice so faint I could barely hear it. 'I got sick with some contagious bug and I ended up in hospital.' I pressed the receiver to my ear. It sounded like he was ringing from the middle of a sandstorm. ' . . . All the while I was lying there no one was allowed near me to visit

270

. . . *crackle, crackle, crackle* . . . I just kept thinking that if you were there you would have made it into that room . . . *crackle, crackle, crackle* . . . You wouldn't have taken no for an answer from anyone, and it made me think . . . Jo, we should get married.'

Even though he was 6,000 miles away, the words hit me like a thunderbolt. It was a phrase I had dreamed of hearing. The thought of someone wanting to spend their life with me through sickness and health, all that stuff. It was overwhelming.

'I've been thinking about it,' he continued, before I could answer. 'My parents have said that if you want to leave the fire service and travel with me they'll give us an income of £400 a month. We could travel the world together.' I hadn't needed much persuading, but that was the icing on the cake. I heard myself say 'Yes'.

He carried on talking, but I hardly heard his words. Thoughts swirled through my mind, coming too fast and from too many directions for me to process them. I was getting married! And I was leaving the fire service, too. I was giving up everything I'd worked for to travel through the Amazon with a Foreign Legionnaire. My head was spinning so much I felt sick. As we said a long, loving goodbye, the sandstorm of static in the background became louder than ever. By the time I eventually put the receiver down, it sounded more like a hurricane.

21

White Wedding

Everyone agreed it had been a fairytale wedding. A dress made from ivory silk, organza and Chantilly lace, bridesmaids in peach taffeta, and a classically handsome groom dressed in top hat and tails. There was no doubt about it. The marriage of Scott and Charlene from *Neighbours* would undoubtedly be the television highlight of 1988. My nuptials the year before, however, were rather different.

I'd never wanted a big wedding and was secretly pleased that David had left all the planning and organization to me. I couldn't think of anything worse than some cheesy ceremony with bridesmaids, bouquets and a tiered wedding cake — it was all way too feminine for me.

Because it was at such short notice, I'd booked the register office in Watton for 10 a.m. on Saturday, 19 December. David had only arrived back in the UK a few days earlier, looking thin, tired and travel weary, and I'd barely seen him since.

The day was cold and miserable and we wore outfits to match — both in grey. There were twelve people at the ceremony, and once the paperwork was done, we walked around the corner to the restaurant I'd booked. It was closed. It had started to rain, so to kill time until it opened we sat in Greggs the bakers drinking cups of tea, much to the amusement of the regulars.

After the meal and a few drinks, David and I were driven back to Melford Common in a white car, decked out with balloons, tinsel and ribbons. It was cold and dark by the time we arrived home, and we were in bed before midnight. I really didn't mind, because all I could think about was the trip. As the days ticked by towards our departure date, practically all our time was spent poring over the Lonely Planet guide to South America, mapping out our itinerary.

My excitement levels were through the roof. Thanks to the generosity of David's parents we could travel for as long as we wanted, on a joint monthly stipend of £400. To give myself some peace of mind, I'd rented out Melford Common to guarantee I still had some money coming in, and put all my belongings in storage, ready for me when I got back. It all felt too good to be true — like something out of one of my mother-in-law's Mills & Boon novels. We were riding off into the sunset, where we would live happily ever after. Barbara Cartland, eat your heart out!

Our plan was to spend a couple of months travelling across Brazil, before heading into Peru to visit Machu Picchu before hooking up with his contacts — a team from Oxford University who were conducting drug trials in the High Andes. The area was very dangerous, he explained — kidnappings were par for the course. We'd then head into Bolivia, Colombia and Ecuador, boarding a cargo boat at the port of Guayaquil before moving into Central America. From there, we would go where the fancy took us, criss-crossing the United States until, at some far distant date, we returned home. As we scoured the pages, making notes and fantasizing about how fabulous it was all going to be, I knew I was hooked on wanderlust. We both were.

I had to pinch myself each morning to convince myself it was true. I loved being a firefighter more than anything, but I was ecstatic to think I would be exchanging my mornings scrubbing the wheel arches of the pump for adventures in the Amazon.

I'd filled a rucksack with all the essentials I'd need for the trip, and sewn a small Union

Jack patch next to the zip. Apart from the flag, I realized, everything in it was exactly the same as David's. I thought back to the day I'd collected my fire service uniform at Whitegates. Now, it seemed, I had another wardrobe and identity — as Mrs Blakeney. This certainly had its advantages. My new husband was as tough as they come — a walking insurance policy. He wasn't scared of anything or anybody. Truth be told, I was more worried for the welfare of the locals. David was also, he assured me, fluent in the 'gutter' Spanish he'd picked up in the Legion, meaning that we'd be able to get by on our travels without any problem.

The only hurdle remaining before I embarked on my new life was my last day at work — 8 January 1988. By some strange coincidence, it was exactly a year on from Chris's death. Was my scruffy angel up there looking out for me? I prayed that he was.

★ ★ ★

'As you all know, I'm not a great one for public speaking. However, as this is Jo's last day with us I thought I should say a few words . . . ' I was standing in the lecture room listening to Nigel give the speech I never thought I'd hear.

I'd been busying myself with my usual daily tasks when his voice boomed over the tannoy, ordering me to the lecture room. On entering, I'd come face to face with a sea of smiling faces. Practically everyone I'd ever worked with was there, standing in a semi-circle beneath a banner reading 'Good-bye Jungle Jo — We're Going To Miss You'.

'Despite her love of the fire service, Jo's leaving us for a new life roughin' it and toughin' it in the Amazon,' said Nigel as I took my place at the front of the crowd. 'The news has come as a shock to all of us, and I for one will be very sorry to see her go. However, I think we can all agree it's an amazing opportunity, and one that none of us would pass up, given the chance.' He gestured for me to join him on the small dais. 'As a small token of our appreciation, I'd like to present her with this parting gift, and, on behalf of everyone here at Thetford, wish her the very best of luck in the future.'

Everyone clapped as I ripped open the neatly wrapped parcel. It was a top-of-the-range Victorinox Swiss army knife, complete with scissors, saw, magnifying glass and a hundred other useful tools. It was so big it barely fitted in my hand. I really didn't know what to say.

'How about 'Thanks'?' hollered Andy.

'At least the bottle opener will get some use,' added Ronnie.

'Have they got branches of Oddbins in the Amazon?' queried Trevor.

Christ, I was going to miss them. Looking around at these familiar faces, memories of the experiences we'd shared flooded through my mind. The firework displays where we'd shoot Roman Candles into the night sky from giant mortars, the noise so loud it rattled the windows; the drunken fancy dress parties; the brutal games of 'Sponge' with Trevor in the pump bay. Then there was the job itself. I'd loved every pulse-quickening second when we were out on shouts. Nothing could beat it. But I'd enjoyed the bread-and-butter stuff, too — rescuing cats from trees, cutting rings off fingers, freeing little boys who had got their heads stuck in railings.

From the minute I'd gazed into that display cabinet at Whitegates and seen the eight-pointed star of the Norfolk Fire Service, I'd known what I wanted. It had provided me with a code of conduct, a path to follow and, unexpectedly, friends for life.

But now I was saying goodbye. The big, bad world outside of Thetford's walls suddenly felt very real. When I'd been clearing out my locker I'd found Graeme's 'Different Day, Same Shit' badge. Was I going to miss the routine? My stomach lurched. I couldn't tell if it was from excitement or anxiety.

I was jolted back into reality by the sight of Nigel walking towards me with two cups of tea. Everyone had broken off into small groups, and he motioned towards a quiet corner of the mess room. 'It's been a pleasure working with you, Jo,' he said, picking the tobacco from his teeth as he lit another licorice roll-up. I was going to miss that smell. ' . . . Apart from the electrocution, obviously.'

We drank our tea in companionable silence. It seemed like a lifetime since I'd first arrived at Thetford and sat in his office, green as grass. He'd been the best teacher I'd ever had. I opened my mouth to say as much, knowing the words would come out clichéd, but he cut me off. 'Oh well,' he said, winking at me as he stood up, 'back to the grindstone.'

I watched him walk over to where the rest of the guys were standing. As usual they were laughing, joking and shooting the breeze. It was almost lunchtime, and a delicious aroma wafted through from the kitchen. 'What's on the menu, Mary?' I heard him say, as, in a cloud of licorice, the door closed behind him.

It was the perfect goodbye. I collected my things from my locker, hung up my firefighter's uniform and walked out of the front door into the bright January sunshine.

There was a new adventure ahead of me, and I couldn't wait to get started.

Acknowledgements

I have lots of people to thank. First of all, my mother, my cause to rebel against. I can't help but love you. Malcolm, for being my constant and for maintaining our little support group as we head into our fifties and beyond.

It's been quite a journey to get here. A few years ago, a friend called Martyn Goodacre, a brilliant photographer, suggested that I write a book. Together with his best buddy, writer Paul Moody, they got the project started. This book wouldn't exist without you both. Thank you for pushing me again and again!

I'd also like to thank my friends in the Norfolk Fire Service for helping me on this trip down memory lane. A special thank you to Nigel Monument, my old boss, Trevor Leggett for reminding me who I am, and Andy Bates for making me cry with laughter as I chatted to him about the past. A very special thanks, too, to Chief Fire Officer Hogg. What an incredibly brave decision you and your team took to employ me — I hope I didn't let you down. Thanks also to Colin Farrington, my HGV driving instructor. To me, all these people are heroes. I'd also like to, thank the folks at Whitegates, who were so kind and helpful (especially Bettina Herbert). I'm delighted to report it still has that impressive air of grandeur and purpose.

This book is also in loving memory of my father, Neil Dallas and Chris Lancaster.

We do hope that you have enjoyed reading this large print book.

Did you know that all of our titles are available for purchase?

We publish a wide range of high quality large print books including:
Romances, Mysteries, Classics
General Fiction
Non Fiction and Westerns

Special interest titles available in large print are:
The Little Oxford Dictionary
Music Book
Song Book
Hymn Book
Service Book

Also available from us courtesy of Oxford University Press:
Young Readers' Dictionary
(large print edition)
Young Readers' Thesaurus
(large print edition)

For further information or a free brochure, please contact us at:
Ulverscroft Large Print Books Ltd.,
The Green, Bradgate Road, Anstey,
Leicester, LE7 7FU, England.
Tel: (00 44) **0116 236 4325**
Fax: (00 44) **0116 234 0205**

DAUGHTER MOTHER ME

Alana Kirk

In life, women can have many labels: daughter, wife, career woman, mother. Alana Kirk has worn them all; and, whilst her life is hectic, she feels in control. Then, four days after the birth of her third daughter, her mother suffers a massive stroke. And just like that, everything changes . . . Alana has entered what she terms her 'Sandwich Years' — sandwiched between seeing to the needs of her parents and children: both grieving for, and caring for, her beloved mum; supporting her father; raising her three young daughters; and getting her career back on track. But how long can she continue before the cracks begin to show?